D1011338

Armed Robbery

Crime and Society Series

Series editor: Hazel Croall

Published titles
Sex Crime, by Terry Thomas
Burglary, by R. I. Mawby
Armed Robbery, by Roger Matthews

Armed Robbery

Roger Matthews

WILLAN
PUBLISHING

Published by

Willan Publishing
Culmcott House
Mill Street, Uffculme
Cullompton, Devon
EX15 3AT, UK
Tel: +44(0)1884 840337
Fax: +44(0)1884 840251
e-mail: info@willanpublishing.co.uk
website: www.willanpublishing.co.uk

Published simultaneously in the USA and Canada by

Willan Publishing
c/o ISBS, 5824 N.E. Hassalo St,
Portland, Oregon 97213-3644, USA
Tel: +001(0)503 287 3093
Fax: +001(0)503 280 8832
e-mail: info@isbs.com
website: www.isbs.com

© Roger Matthews 2002

All rights reserved; no part of this publication may be reproduced, stored in a retrieval
system, or transmitted in any form or by any means, electronic, mechanical,
photocopying, recording or otherwise without the prior written permission of the
Publishers or a licence permitting copying in the UK issued by the Copyright Licensing
Agency Ltd, 90 Tottenham Court Road, London W1P 9HE.

First published 2002

ISBN 1-903240-60-3 Paperback
ISBN 1-903240-61-1 Hardback

British Library Cataloguing-in-Publication Data
A catalogue record for this book is available from the British Library.

Printed by T J International Ltd, Trecerus Industrial Estate, Padstow, Cornwall
Typeset by PDQ Typesetting, Newcastle-under-Lyme, Staffordshire

Contents

Figures and tables

Figures

Tables

Acknowledgements

There is a considerable number of people who have contributed in different ways to the production of this book. In particular, I would like to thank DCI Steve Talbot of the South Yorkshire Police, Commander Bill Griffiths and DC Alan Townsend of the Flying Squad, together with the various officers in both these forces who agreed to be interviewed. I would like to thank the Prisons Department for allowing access to different prisons and to the prison staff who arranged interviews with convicted armed robbers. In particular, I would like to thank the 340 armed robbers who took part in the interviews.

Thanks also go to Peter Francis and Peter Devereaux who conducted a number of the interviews with prisoners, as well as to Dr Martin Gill for helping with the design of the questionnaires and the interviewing of robbers. Other people who have contributed in different ways include Julie Bains, Ken Pease, Mick Creedon, John Bryan, Andrew Stoll, Ruth Jamieson and Catriona Woolner.

A particular word of thanks go to Joe Cohen, who played a critical role in resolving a dispute over copyright, and to Dr Terry Butland, who supported my endeavours.

Roger Matthews
Middlesex University
January 2002

Chapter 1

Methodology, data and sources

Although armed robbery is widely considered to be one of the most serious of crimes (carrying a long prison sentence and subject to a considerable amount of media attention), there is very little academic research on the subject. There have, of course, been a number of popular books written on notorious robberies such as the Brinks-Matt and the Great Train robberies as well as commentaries on the 'underworld', but very little attention has been paid, particularly in Britain, to a crime that has been defined as 'the taking of goods or money by actual or threatened force.'[1] The aim of this book is to fill this gap in knowledge and to contribute to a more detailed understanding of this issue.

Two major research projects were conducted between 1992 and 1998 that provide the primary data on which this book is based. Material is also drawn from a wide range of secondary sources and related studies from around the world which have, in different ways, contributed to an important but muted international debate. The first of these two pieces of research was carried out between 1992 and 1995 and involved interviews with approximately 340 convicted armed robbers in 12 different English prisons. The prisons selected included mainly high-security dispersal prisons but a number of different types of prison establishments were visited, including two young offenders institutions.

The research in prisons was funded by the British Bankers' Association and the Building Societies Association who were concerned at the time about an increase in armed robberies and wanted to find out something about robbers' motivation, the selection of targets and the effectiveness of different crime prevention strategies. The banks and building societies were experimenting with rising screens, double-entry doors and more sophisticated forms of video surveillance, and they wanted to know whether these measures were likely to make any difference to offender motivation. The second research project was conducted between 1994 and 1996 and was funded by the Home Office Police Research Group. It was selected as a response to the prioritisation of armed robbery by the Association of Chief Police Officers (ACPO) Crime Strategy Group. There was a growing concern at this time with offences involving firearms along with a recognition that, despite the serious nature of the offence, little was known about the effectiveness of different police strategies around the country. The aim of this research was to examine police methods and, in particular, to compare the approaches of a dedicated robbery unit, in this case the Flying Squad, with a non-dedicated CID unit in South Yorkshire. Interviews were also conducted with different police units responsible for armed robbery in Manchester and Nottingham.

In both these pieces of research the normal procedures were followed. Questionnaires were constructed and detailed consideration was given to the range and depth of the questions to be asked. The prisons-based research was arranged through the Prisons Department and although this was a slow process, it guaranteed a reasonable level of co-operation from prison officials. A number of prisons were identified, mostly category A and dispersal prisons as well as a number of young offender institutions. In each prison lists of armed robbers were found in the LIDS (Local Index Data System) index and the prison authorities distributed a standard letter that was addressed to those whose current sentence was for armed robbery, inviting them to participate in an interview. Responses were collected and the prison authorities arranged interviews with those prisoners who had agreed. Each prison was visited in turn and the research went smoothly except that we had underestimated how short the available time for conducting interviews was in the prison since we were only allowed to conduct interviews for two and half hours in the morning 9.30 a.m. – 12.00 p.m. and from 2.30 to 4.00 p.m. in the afternoon. Although the prison day can be extremely long for prisoners it is relatively short for interviewers. By the time we had gone through security and found somewhere to carry out the interviews, it was often 10.30 in the morning before the interviews could actually start. Finding a suitable space for conducting interviews in often overcrowded prisons proved to be difficult and time consuming (Martin 2000).

Interviews, where possible, were recorded and later transcribed. In cases in which prisoners did not agree to the interviews being recorded or in the few cases in which the prison authorities objected, detailed notes were taken during the interview. Those who agreed to participate in the interviews were asked about their offending histories, their entry into armed robbery, the selection of targets and victims, use of firearms, relations with the police and their experience of the criminal justice process. In cases where it was suspected that responses may have been consciously distorted or exaggerated, checks were made against available information on particular prisoners. Where there were found to be inconsistencies between the response given and the available information, the interviews were discarded. Interviews lasted on average around 45 minutes but, in some cases in which respondents were particularly forthcoming and provided informative detailed accounts, the interviews could last two or three hours.

Conducting the research with the police proved to be easier in terms of access. Because the research was funded by the Police Research Group in the Home Office and because the ACPO had prioritised this issue, setting up the research was relatively straightforward. This research was based on a study of sample of cases in the London area, and a review of all the armed robbery cases over the previous year in South Yorkshire, by going through the case reports. A selection of these cases was then followed up through interviews with the officers involved in the selected cases in order to gain a better understanding of the policing strategies involved in dealing with different cases. In all, the sample from the Metropolitan Police District (MPD) involved 235 cases selected out of a total of 1,193, while South Yorkshire involved some 165 cases, which was the total number of recorded armed robberies during 1993. Of the MPD cases examined, approximately half had 'successful' outcomes in that the offender was arrested and charged. The aim was to examine the methods that had been employed to deal with reported armed robberies in order to determine the role and effectiveness of different approaches. The MPD cases were divided as evenly as possible between the four branches of the Flying Squad, with 51 located in Finchley, 63 in Barnes, 63 in Rigg Approach and 58 in Tower Bridge. The analysis also drew upon interviews with police officers of different ranks, relevant documentation, data relating to recorded crime and clear-up rates, and secondary literature relating to armed robbery, both locally and nationally.

The fieldwork was carried out mainly during 1994–95. At this time both forces were undergoing restructuring and reorganisation. This had both positive and negative implications for the research. On the positive side it raised a number of issues in officers' minds about alternative operational and organisational methods to deal with armed robbery. On the negative side, restructuring brought a degree of uncertainty, which made some officers apprehensive and reluctant to express critical comments since it was feared these might feed into the reassessment exercise and produce undesirable consequences for the unit.

The main objective was to examine the approach of a dedicated unit (the Flying Squad) based in London and a CID unit based in South

3

Yorkshire to see if there were any advantages in a having a dedicated robbery unit. The questions asked of the police centred on identifying different methods of investigation and detection, the use of informants, the surveillance of suspects, the mobilisation of evidence, the use of firearms and the process of prosecution. The examination of police methods was designed to compare the effectiveness of proactive and reactive strategies, to assess the ways in which information was gathered and disseminated, to examine relative clear-up rates and to investigate the deployment of firearms, as well as the use of armed response vehicles. In both the interviews with convicted armed robbers in prison and with the police, the primary focus was on what are generally seen as the more serious forms of armed robberies, or what the police refer to as 'Band 1' robberies. These involve robberies against banks, building societies, betting shops, post offices, jewellers and cash-in-transit. Other types of commercial premises, such as shops, garages, off-licences and offices, are referred top as 'Band 2' targets. Because of the relatively low level of Band 1 robberies in South Yorkshire both Band 1 and Band 2 robberies were included in the survey. The terms 'Band 1' and 'Band 2' are a little cumbersome and make assumptions about the 'seriousness' of different types of commercial robbery that are not always correct. However, we have used these terms in the course of our investigation because they do provide a way, however crude, of distinguishing between different sets of targets.

Both pieces of research went relatively smoothly and the designated research strategies were closely followed. The research was completed, the findings written up and analysed. The selection of research methods was generally vindicated and the findings were disseminated in the usual ways (Gill and Matthews 1994). But on reflection what was interesting about the research was the informal processes and the less visible dynamics of the research process. In fact, it became apparent that the success, or otherwise, of research of this kind is as much dependent upon the flexibility, adaptability and imagination of the researchers as it is on the original research design. Surprisingly, much research is written up without any reference to these critical, but less visible, processes, despite the fact they can have a major impact on the nature and quality of the research.

It became apparent in the course of the research that it was deeply influenced by a number of factors. These factors included the social class, gender, age and ethnicity of the researchers. In both projects the researchers were all male, drawn from the 'respectable' working class, white and aged between 20 and 40 years. Importantly in this respect, they generally overlapped with the demographic characteristics of the population being interviewed. Over 90 per cent of convicted armed robbers are male, come from poorer inner-city areas and are in the 20–40 years age group. Similarly with the police, although they are likely to be drawn from the more respectable sections of the working class, they have a similar social demographic profile as the researchers. The class and gender affinities and understandings were critical in developing the research. It is not that middle-class female researchers would not have been able to carry out research on this topic but that it would almost certainly be a very different type of project in which the understandings, meanings and affinities would be transformed.

Just as research on domestic violence has shown that employing female researchers to interview female victims makes an enormous difference to the quality and type of information elicited because of the level of empathy and understandings involved, so the same logic applies to this research (Mooney 1993). In a similar vein, Elaine Genders and Elaine Player (1995) noted in their research on Grendon Prison that being relatively young and attractive female researchers in an overwhelmingly male environment influenced deeply the way in which they conducted the research, and may have influenced their findings. The gender component is ever present and, although its effects may be fairly subtle, it can nevertheless exercise a major impact on the outcome of the research. There is no gender-neutral research. However, as Genders and Players (ibid.) have pointed out, the apparent disadvantages of being female in a male prison can be turned to advantage. Although they were perceived by senior staff as a security risk and were aware that amongst some inmates they became the objects of sexual fantasies, they found they were able to overcome the defensiveness of some prisoners by encouraging them to discuss their personal problems as a way of entering into a discussion about their offending behaviour.

Besides the gender component there is an important class dimension to the research. As Dick Hobbs (1989) pointed out in his study of East End entrepreneurship and policing, his own working-class background, accent and language were a critical component in building up a rapport with his subjects and establishing a necessary level of trust. Similarly Janet Foster (1990), in her study of 'villains' in south London, found she needed to spend a considerable amount of time in the locality in order to build up credibility amongst the local population, particularly given her middle-class accent.

It also became abundantly clear that *trust* is a fundamental requirement for conducting detailed investigative research, particularly with deviant and marginalised populations. Having a similar, or at least overlapping, linguistic repertoire with the population being studied can be a critical element in establishing a necessary degree of trust. Alongside linguistic affinities, the demeanour and the body language of the researcher can be important in establishing a basis for communication. Convicted offenders may be educationally underachievers but they are not stupid. They are quick to identify the nuances of language. They pick up the cues and they interpret the signs. They know you are an academic. They know you have the approval of the Prisons Department and the co-operation of the 'screws'. You come with a health warning. They may be intrigued but they are understandably suspicious. In one wing of Dartmoor the word was put around we were the police trying to gather information and improve clear-ups. Needless to say we did not carry out any interviews on that wing. In other places prisoners were suspicious we were somehow linked to the psychology department and that we were part of a personality assessment or risk assessment exercise. In these cases some of the prisoners felt quite relieved and reassured when we told them we were funded by the banks and building societies and were trying to help them prevent robberies.

One response to the problem of establishing trust and a rapport with prospective interviewees is to spend a considerable amount of time in the research situation in order to become accepted as part of the 'community' (see King and McDermott 1995; Sparks *et al* 1996). This option was not really open to us in prisons since we had contracted at the outset to conduct a large number of interviews in a relatively limited period of time. However, on reflection it may have been preferable to have carried out fewer interviews and to have spent more time both formally and informally in the prisons we visited. We found that using quite a lengthy semi-structured questionnaire with approximately 340 respondents meant that, given the time constraints on researchers in prison, there was growing pressure to complete them in time. It was the case, however, that we encountered diminishing returns in that the interviews started to become repetitive and less informative after a while and often we did not have the time to probe into the more interesting areas of discussion. This is in part because our interests and priorities changed in the course of doing the research. Some of the things we felt were vitally important at the outset declined in significance in the course of the research and other issues caught our attention. This is hardly surprising since the literature on armed robbery, which we had consulted beforehand, is extremely limited and narrowly focused. Consequently, we had not been fully sensitised to a number of potentially interesting issues. Moreover, the research process itself should be a learning experience for the researcher who reflects upon the issues, asks different questions in the light of findings and develops the problematic. As new research questions emerged attempts were made to create more space and to investigate them within the interview schedule. Amongst the themes that came to take up more time in the interviews were the use and acquisition of firearms, the nature of organised crime and its relation to armed robbery, and the relation between armed robbery and drugs.

A more serious limitation on the prisons-based research, however, became apparent some time after the research had been completed. This related not so much to the more factual information on the selection of targets or the organisation of particular robberies, but to the more personal questions about attitudes and values. The convicted armed robbers were asked (amongst other things) for their views on violence, firearms, victims and the operation of the criminal justice system. At the time we took most of these responses at face value. But looking back and analysing the data it became increasingly apparent that many of the responses were 'learned' and that the attitudes of remorse and regret that were frequently expressed were part of a repertoire of responses that had been developed in prison. It was significant, for example, that the vast majority of respondents played down the benefits or attractiveness of armed robbery and instead explained their involvement predominantly in terms of a need for money or because of unfortunate circumstances. However, it is evident in many of the accounts of active armed robbers that they see their activities in a very different light and, in fact, tend to present themselves as very different types of people.

In Laurie Taylor's perceptive depiction of the London underworld (1985), the villains he describes display different attitudes towards crime and justice than we found amongst the majority of imprisoned armed robbers. For example, in his description of an incident in which John McVicar gave a lecture to a large group of probation officers, he notes that:

At the end of the talk one of them stood up and congratulated him on the book (*McVicar by Himself*). This, he said, he had found very moving. It had greatly helped him to understand why John became involved in crime, and his struggle to overcome his criminal predilections. However he had detected in the film (*McVicar*) a much cruder approach. In the film he merely seemed to be enjoying, himself when he was out robbing banks and on the run. How could he explain the difference? Was the film untrue?

'Well,' John replied, not I suspect, without a certain enjoyment, 'That's exactly as it should have been. Because, you see, the book with all its accounts of childhood and causes was written originally as my defence statement, when I had been picked up again after the escape. It was really written for people like probation officers. So I

7

am glad you liked it. The film, on the other hand, was a bit more about how it really was' (ibid.: 129).

In general Laurie Taylor's account of the lives and attitudes of the villains operating in the 'underworld' conveys a sense of excitement and satisfaction about their involvement in serious crime. It was indicative, however, that in a number of interviews after a few remarks about what a pathetic and unrewarding crime armed robbery was, various robbers would start to become more animated when they described their various exploits and conquests. One robber called George, who was interviewed in Dartmoor and who had grown up in Bethnal Green in the Krays' 'manor', for example, was fairly subdued during the interview but became more excited when describing the crime for which he had been sent to prison.

George had carried out a major robbery at a country house with his accomplice, Bill. The job had been set up by an undisclosed third party who worked for an insurance company. It transpired his company had been asked to insure a number of valuable antiques, most of which had been bought from major London auction houses. George and Bill carried out a brief inspection of the property under the guise of being from the water board and they confirmed that the items they sought were in fact in the house. They returned at a later date, gagged and bound the staff who were on duty, and then loaded the designated merchandise on to a container truck. They drove the truck to Heathrow and put the container in storage. Having secured their haul (which they reckoned to be worth around £2.5 million according to the catalogue price), they were paid £200,000 between them by the person who had set the job up, and immediately decided to celebrate.

George and Bill, as it happens, had recently met two women from Oxford and arranged to go to see them over the weekend. They acquired a suitably stylish car and purchased a selection of alcoholic beverages, as well as a ridiculously large quantity of cocaine. They motored up the A40, music blaring out of the car, windows down, swigging beer and snorting coke, while singing along to the state-of-the-art car stereo system. They were full of drink, drugs and desire. This was the moment. This was what it was all about. This, in short, was heaven. However, as they approached a roundabout on the A40 there was a police car coming on to the roundabout from another road. Bill, who was driving, waved them on, and the police in turn indicated they should go first. Bill, being in a particularly benign frame of mind, saw this as a rare act of politeness by the police and went round the roundabout. They continued along the A40 still singing, drinking and snorting. About five or ten minutes later

Bill and George spontaneously looked at each other in dismay. They had both realised at exactly the same moment, even through the haze of euphoria, that there was now no traffic in front or behind them as far as they could see. Why were they now on the road alone? The answer came suddenly when they saw a number of police cars approaching from every direction with lights flashing, sirens blaring and tyres screeching. It was game over.

This account highlighted the uncertain, capricious and hedonistic world many of the imprisoned armed robbers appear to have inhabited previously. It was one of a number of stories and anecdotes that spilled out in the course of the interviews. It conveyed graphically something of the excitement and pleasure that were obviously a significant part of their lives before they had been caught and imprisoned. There were other more mundane stories of luxury holidays, parties, extravagant purchases and various binges that would follow a successful robbery.

So there is a need to exercise some caution when interviewing prisoners since there is a tendency to lose sight of the initial seduction of crime (Katz 1988). In individual and group discussions in prison, prisoners may learn to play down the initial attractiveness of crime and to rationalise their involvement. However, as Richard Wright and Scott Decker argue (1997: 4):

Much criminal behaviour is a direct response to the pressures and temptations of life on the streets. Prisoners are insulated from these powerful forces – are no longer under their spell – and thus may respond quite differently from how they would in the outside world. What is more, it is clear that the accounts offered by incarcerated offenders often are distorted by the prison environment. No matter how much inmates are assured otherwise, many will continue to believe what they say to researchers will get back to the authorities and influence their chances for early release. And even if this does not seem likely, why take the chance? Consequently, inmates are inclined to put the best possible spin on their previous criminal activities. Further, the experience of being apprehended and punished can alter how prisoners retro-actively perceive the actions that brought about their downfall.

The question Wright and Decker raise is this: why should prisoners participate in research? Clearly, it would be naive to believe they have any real interest in advancing academic research on armed robbery or helping to further the development of crime prevention measures. So why would these prisoners agree to participate in these interviews? We

9

might suggest three reasons. First, participation in interviews provides a break from the boredom and monotony of prison life. Secondly, some prisoners are inquisitive or want to be part of whatever is going on. Thirdly, they may think there might be some personal advantage in showing a willingness to participate in the research and in taking the opportunity to discuss and reflect upon their misdemeanours.

Therefore there are not only the intrinsic difficulties of carrying out fieldwork within the physical and social constraints of these segregative institutions but these constraints themselves are also generally compounded by an underlying sense of multiple and shifting realities (Sparks *et al* 1996; King 2000). The context of prison research is critical in framing the relation between researcher and respondent, in determining what is said and how it can be said. In short, reality on the inside occurs in a unique time and space in which meanings and identities can change (Matthews 1999).

During the interview imprisoned armed robbers, like other interviewees, will tend to tell you what they think you want to hear, or at least tell you what is most convenient or least harmful for them. In some prisons we were met by prisoners who felt they had been wrongfully confined and who thought we might be able to help with their case. When they found out we were not able to help they disappeared. Similarly on one of the wings in Parkhurst a number of armed robbers claimed they had been set up by the Flying Squad with the help of a known villain who had arranged various robberies. These robberies they claimed, had been organised by the police, who were waiting to arrest the robbers, making sure the person who set up the robbery disappeared from the scene. From the police's point of view this was an effective, if dubious, way of catching known villains with limited resources, while helping to improve the clear-up rate. These prisoners were not claiming they were not involved in armed robbery but they were complaining about entrapment. Most of them were serving sentences of between 8 and 15 years. Again, there was little or nothing we could do but to note that the grievances and most of the interviews on this particular wing centred around complaints about 'unfair' police tactics.[2]

The interviews were not without their lighter moments. We heard some bizarre cases and of the strange circumstances that were associated with offenders being caught. For example, there were two robbers who had passed notes over the counter demanding money that had their name and address or some means of identification on the other side. There was another case where a middle-aged man with no previous convictions for robbery had carried out an attack on a building society in order to impress his estranged wife and win her back. After he gave her all the money from the robbery, which was in the region of £1,000, she turned him in to the police. Another case involved the planned co-operation of a security officer who, however, was unknown personally to the robber. Unfortunately for them, the shifts were unexpectedly changed with the consequence that the robber arrived expecting to meet a friendly face but instead met belligerent security staff who did not realise the robber's aggressive gestures were play acting. They fought him to the ground, forcibly restrained him and then called the police to arrest him.

At the same time there were some robbers who understood and operated sophisticated electronic communications equipment and had been involved in robberies requiring detailed and intricate planning. Clearly, the armed robbers who were interviewed were not an homogeneous group. Within the broad social demographic character-istics which the majority shared, there were significant variations in attitudes, abilities and experience.

It was also evident that the majority of the people who agreed to be interviewed were not, by and large, those at the top of the profession. That is, most of the convicted armed robbers we interviewed were at the middle and lower end of the continuum, with a few notable exceptions. In Parkhurst Special Unit, for example, two armed robbers who were described to us by the prison officers as two of the most dangerous men in the country agreed to be interviewed at length. One was Italian who had recently written a book himself about his exploits (Viccei 1992).[3] He invited us to drink cappuccino (made from a sachet) and told us that, when he first arrived in England, he could hardly speak any English and that his girlfriend used to write the demand notes which were to be shown to the bank clerks on pieces of card. This worked reasonably well as long as the bank clerks did not want to engage in any kind of verbal exchange.

The second armed robber interviewed in the special unit was a Robert Redford look-alike who boasted of always having a £500,000 float when working and of frightening security staff so much they normally threw him the keys to the van and ran away. In one incident in which he was cornered he had shot three policeman in the legs and had received a sentence of 22 years. Both were locked up in this small enclosed unit in which proper daylight is excluded by the window coverings, while the thick walls are wired and alarmed. On any one day the number of officers on duty will normally exceed the number of inmates. The bulk of respondents, however, could not match these credentials. Instead, they held positions lower down the criminal hierarchy, although in general within the prison armed robbers are considered towards the top of the prison pecking order by both prisoners and staff.

Despite all theses provisos and caveats the sample of convicted armed robbers was in general research terms very large, and a reasonable percentage had interesting things to say. The difficulty for the researcher was distinguishing between those things that were genuine and those that were said because respondents thought it was what we wanted to hear or because they thought it would present a better picture of their activities to the authorities. There was also a relatively low level of response from ethnic minority groups, probably because they suspected we would be white, middle-class academics. We did not make any special attempt to attract ethnic minority offenders. In contrast, we did try to locate and interview women armed robbers but, despite considerable efforts, almost every time we located someone we were told they were 'unavailable' or were just about to be transferred to another prison. Consequently, we were only able to interview one woman.

It might be argued the research strategy that was employed, and the processes of self-selection of respondents, means the research is not representative or objective. However, since the social and demographic characteristics of the existing population of armed robbers are unknown, combined with the fact that the prison population itself involves a pre-selected population, the objective was not to search for a generally representative sample. Rather, the intention was to recognise the specific nature of the population included and to note the obvious omissions in order to acknowledge the limits to possible generalisations. This in itself does not make the research any less 'objective' or 'scientific'. The point of all scientific inquiry, as Andrew Sayer (1992: 252) has argued, is not to develop a spurious representativeness but is rather 'to change and develop our understanding and reduce illusion'.

Although the research was carried out within the closed confines of the prison it was like other forms of social research, 'open' and subject to interpretation, change and educational effects. Social research that aims to remain connected to its object of inquiry must be flexible and continuously negotiated with adjustments being made in the light of the research experience itself. As Bhaskar (1975) has argued, even the most straightforward laboratory-based research is 'manipulated' by the researcher. An awareness of the negotiated and changeable nature of the process and the educational effects of intervention and social change suggests that much social research is in effect a form of 'action research'. Recognising the prevalence of these processes should make us more flexible and less rigid about conducting social research, with the expectation that whilst the research strategy may guide the research the tactics of implementation may well need to be revised regularly in the process. The implication of this observation is that the quality of the research is dependent not only on the formulation of an appropriate methodology but will be also call upon the resourcefulness, experience and abilities of the researchers.

The second tier of the research involved interviews with members of the Flying Squad in London and the CID in South Yorkshire. This aspect of the research raised another set of methodological issues, which were very different from those we had met in prison but were no less challenging. The significance of interviewing the police raises all the questions of conducting research amongst professional agencies. At first sight conducting such research appears more straightforward. However, new issues arise for the researcher, for here we had to operate in a more tightly structured bureaucratic environment in which individuals, however polite and welcoming they may appear, have a vested interest in protecting and promoting the agency.

The main problems of penetrating this particular bureaucratic organisation were first, gaining access and getting co-operation and, second, identifying the relevant data. Much of the police data was not computerised but kept in log-books and card files. Also, there is generally a 'need to know' policy in operation by which the police ensure researchers are only given the information the police feel they need to know. Information is rarely volunteered. This means there is a continual process of prodding and fishing for information. Sometimes the police are deliberately obstructive, as we found when trying to get information on informers, but most of the time there is a careful filtering of information. Since the police research was funded by the Home Office and sanctioned indirectly by ACPO, there was a relatively high degree of formal co-operation. We were given access to the files, and prosecuting officers made themselves available to check the details and fill in the blanks. Since one of the researchers was an ex-police officer turned academic, or what has been described in the literature as an 'outsider-insider', there were advantages in terms of a working knowledge of police practices, informal culture and jargon (Reiner 1992; Sheptycki 1994). While this insider knowledge proved useful there always tends to be some suspicion however of the motives of those police officers who turn academic researchers.

Although it was no doubt a major advantage that the research on the police was funded by the Police Research Group (PRG), it was apparent from the outset that the predominant focus was to be on issues of cost-effectiveness and identifying good practice. And as such it was to some extent subject to the criticism that has been levelled at most PRG-sponsored research reports, in that they tend to 'avoid the length and theoretical stance of academic deliberations, but are rather written up in an accessible, concise format and are implementable' (Brown 1996: 183). The focus of the research was on the processes of detection and the organisational issues with the clear indication that theoretical and conceptual discussion should be kept to an absolute minimum (see Matthews 1998).

Research on 'cop culture' has emphasised the variation in the perspectives of officers of different ranks, and has drawn attention to the various roles police officers adopt. Variations have also been noted between the different personal styles of different forces in different parts of the country (Holdaway 1983; Reiner 1985). Much of this research makes reference to the suspiciousness of the police not only in relation to possible offenders but also to professional bodies who may cause them 'trouble' or may seek to uncover or challenge their activities (Norris 1989). Those police officers involved in policing armed robbery were what has been defined as the 'action seekers' (Walsh 1977), who generally embrace macho values and who were drawn by the excitement associated with this form of crime fighting. It became evident in the course of the research that there were a number of 'gatekeepers' who had to be negotiated, since they all had some control over access to the available data.

In relation to the Flying Squad there were three gatekeepers who had to be negotiated within Scotland Yard if we were to gain a reasonable understanding of police operations. The first type of gatekeeper was the 'public relations' person, the second was associated with 'political correctness' and the third were the information gatherers.

Our first exposure to the police's dealings with armed robbery was managed by what we might call the 'public relations' person. His role was to present a positive picture of police successes in dealing with armed robbery, showing the bravery and ingenuity of Flying Squad officers as well as their specialist skills and considerable expertise in detecting and prosecuting armed robbers. Reference was made to the range of techniques and sophisticated equipment the police had available to deal with these dangerous offenders. The Flying Squad were presented as a dedicated and committed crime-fighting unit and as the cream of the force and who often went beyond the call of duty and risked their lives in order to apprehend suspects and to protect the public. We were shown videos and given a bundle of printouts containing a range of material, much of which was useful, although the information included was highly selective.

The second form of gatekeeping was centred around the identification of the 'political correctness' of the research as well as our value systems and personal orientation. One of the researchers was invited in to meet the then head of the Flying Squad for an informal chat at around 5 p.m.

on a Friday afternoon. Ostensibly this 'informal chat' was about how he could assist in the research. However, as all researchers know, there is no such thing as an 'informal' interview. After exchanging pleasantries and outlining the aims of the research, the researcher was invited for an after-work drink at the end of a 'hard day'. Clearly, refusing a drink would be seen as being impolite. Half a bottle of scotch later the conversation became more intimate and personal. It was about 'cops and robbers' and 'goodies and baddies'. It was about whose side are you on. The questions that arose in quick succession took the following form: 'Don't you think that convicted armed robbers ought to get longer sentences?' and 'We are too soft on them, aren't we?' The conversation then covered a range of issues designed to find out something about the stated and, particularly, the unstated objectives of the research. The point of this conversation was to ensure we were not hostile to the police and, preferably, that we were sympathetic. They wanted to ensure that, if they gave full co-operation, the information would not be used against them and to make sure we did not have a hidden agenda. This ritual, however, had to be gone through. The researcher made the appropriate noises, nodded in the right places and consequently co-operation was authorised.

This opened the door to the third level of gatekeeping. At the time very little information was kept on computer. Instead it was kept in files, log-books and on cards. The disadvantage of this system has over computerised systems of data retrieval is that it is difficult to find and retrieve information without personal assistance from those who actually collected and filed the data. Since the information from the four branches of the Flying Squad (which are located in Finchley, Tower Bridge, Barnes and Rigg Approach) was collated centrally in New Scotland Yard it was important to develop a good working relationship with the two officers who were responsible for gathering and organising this information. We were fortunate in that we were given the summary data of all 'Band 1' armed robberies handled by the Flying Squad between 1992 and 1994. The data source carried extensive details of the distribution of robberies in London, the nature and location of each incident, the characteristics of offenders, the amounts stolen and the type of weapon used. This data source was very useful in building up a more comprehensive picture of the distribution of robberies over time and provided the basis for the identification of trends as well for the calculation, for example, of repeat victimisation.

To some extent the caution exercised by members of the Flying Squad was a function of the confidentiality of their operation and of the fact that their past had been characterised by various scandals and charges of corruption. They were very concerned to try to put this image behind them and to present themselves as a more effective and accountable organisation at the time of the research. However, shortly after our research was completed some members of the Flying Squad were suspended for alleged corruption (Campbell 1998).

The dynamics of carrying out the research in South Yorkshire were very different. This was not only because the organisational structure was different and the level of armed robbery was much lower but also because one of the senior officers in the South Yorkshire CID was an ex-student who had written his MA dissertation on armed robbery (Talbot 1996). The same officer was our Home Office designated link with the South Yorkshire police and was effective in opening doors and securing a very high degree of co-operation from other members of the South Yorkshire CID. Also, at the same time we were carrying out the research, they had just arrested the so-called 'Kagoul Man' who was suspected of carrying out over one hundred armed robberies in the Midlands and Yorkshire, and this arrest had given them considerable notoriety and prestige (McLeod 1994).

In sum, this book is based upon two substantive research projects as well as drawing freely on a range of secondary data. Like other forms of 'realist' social research, this study aims to reflect the stratified nature of social reality, focusing on the structural and institutional context in which the research is located as well as considerations of the class, gender and biographical influences. There is also a recognition of the differences between the formal methods of research and the less well recognised, but equally important, informal and negotiated aspects of the research process. It also aims to provide 'extensive' and 'intensive' dimensions of research, to present quantitative and qualitative data and to link both macro and micro processes (Sayer 1992; Layder 1993; Pawson and Tilley 1997). Like all research, however, it was not without certain problems and limitations. Clearly, the information collected through the prison interviews has to treated with some caution and it would be naive simply to record this data and then subject it to statistical manipulation in the belief that once the data had been through such a process it would somehow be 'cleaned'. The reality is that it is necessary to sift the information given and to realise that the accounts (particularly of offender motivation) that were given in these interviews were in some cases heavily rationalised and sanitised. Similarly with the police research. The information available was collected by a specific agency, with specific interest for a specific purpose. The funding of the two research projects also influenced its orientation and style. In a perfect world the book would include detailed accounts of active criminals together with material drawn from victims. However, having recognised at least some of the limitations of the material included in this book it nevertheless aspires to be one of the most comprehensive studies of commercial robbery carried out to date.

In the following chapters the book will explore the motivations of those who become involved in different forms of armed robbery and will examine, in particular, the relative influences of drugs, violence, money and the media on their propensity to engage in commercial robbery. Based on a review of robbers' own accounts of how targets are selected, some assessment will be made of the effectiveness of different crime prevention strategies in deflecting or reducing robberies. Attention will also be paid to the use of weapons in the pursuit of robberies, and an attempt will be made to deconstruct the meaning of the key term 'armed' in relation to the pursuit of robberies. The impact of robbery on victims will also be explored in some detail since this aspect of commercial robbery has been largely neglected to date. Drawing on our research that focused on the operation of two police forces in England and Wales who are involved in the detection of commercial robberies, the book contrasts the approaches of a dedicated robbery unit with that of typical CID unit in order to identify the advantages, if any, of specialist robbery units. The process of detection will be examined and the question of what are the most effective ways of policing armed robberies will be explored. In the final chapter there is some discussion and analysis of the dramatic reductions in the number of armed robberies that have taken place in recent years. This chapter examines the relative influence of crime prevention measures and gun controls as well as changes in the style of policing, offender motivation and victim resistance on the level and distribution of commercial robberies.

Notes

1 The official definition of robbery in England and Wales is 'A person is guilty of robbery if he or she steals and immediately before or at any time so doing, and in order to do so, uses force, or puts or seeks to put any person in fear of being then and there subjected to force. In summary robbery is stealing aggravated by violence' (Home Office 1991:1).

2 It was difficult to know what to make of these claims at the time, but the subsequent inquiry into the activities of some Flying Squad officers in 1998 suggests that the claims that a number of robberies had been set up by the police were not entirely without foundation.

3 Valerio Viccei became notorious for carrying out one of the largest commercial robberies in recent years, which was known as the Knightsbridge Safety Deposit Box robbery. He was interviewed in the special unit of Parkhurst Prison and was later transferred to a prison in Italy to finish off the remainder of his sentence. After release in 1999 he continued his criminal career and was shot dead by Italian police officers in 2000 (Carroll and Dodd 2000).

Chapter 2

The motivation of armed robbers

Introduction

When asked the question why he robbed banks, one armed robber reportedly replied: 'because that's where they keep the money.' This answer is both profound in its simplicity and directness and naive inasmuch as it fails to address the main question of why take money from banks rather than from other targets. It also avoids the implicit question of why rob at all. In reality, of course, banks nowadays hold only relatively limited amounts of money and the range of security measures most high-street banks employ makes them anything but an obvious target for the aspiring criminal.

Buried beneath these unanswered questions is the more subtle and difficult question of why robberies of commercial premises these days take the form of walking into a bank or similar premises with a weapon and demanding money from the counter. In previous times 'unlawful withdrawals' from commercial premises took significantly different forms.

A hundred years ago, for example, the preferred method of carrying out robberies against commercial premises was 'smash and grab' raids. Between 1920 and 1960 safe-cracking became more prevalent. However, when deterred by the introduction of sophisticated tumbler locks, villains turned to dynamite to blast the lock open or to remove the safe. Using gelignite, however, had the disadvantage that if not carefully placed it can throw the locks into place, making the safe impossible to open, at least for some time. To combat these inconveniences robbers moved from explosives to cutting devices. The oxyacetylene flame and the thermic lance were adopted by a select group of skilled and persistent robbers who used these devices to cut through the metal casing of the safe (Ostler 1969; Ball *et al* 1978; Walsh 1986a).

By the 1960s the practice of robbery against commercial premises changed from being predominantly a form of craft crime to project crime. That is, the introduction of more robust safes and better locks, combined with the difficulties of mobilising heavy and cumbersome cutting equipment, encouraged robbers to adopt a more direct approach. Increasingly the preferred method of carrying out robberies was to enter the premises during business hours with a firearm – preferably a sawn-off shotgun or a Colt 45 – in order to gain compliance and, if necessary, to shoot open the cash draws. Significantly, according to official figures, the number of commercial robberies recorded by the police in which a firearm was reported to have been used increased in England and Wales from approximately 300 in 1973 to around 1,350 in 1986 (Home Office 1986).

During the 1960s a series of high-profile robberies caught the public's attention and raised the profile of armed robbery. Two robberies in particular – the Great Train Robbery in 1963 and the Brinks-Matt Robbery in 1983 – attracted a great deal of attention. They both became embedded in the public consciousness and became part of criminological folklore through the production of books and films that both vilified and celebrated these events (Read 1978; Darbyshire and Hilliard 1993).

The change of style and orientation reflected in these notorious robberies and the growing number of attacks against banks, shops, post offices and security vehicles represented a change in the nature of risk, the instruments used and, ultimately, it required a different form of motivation. Robberies against commercial premises increasingly became 'armed' robberies in which a real or imitation firearm was employed to threaten cashiers or guards. The development of armed robbery in this way involved a degree of deskilling and democratisation. Robbery was no longer restricted to the exploits of a small group of skilled, dedicated criminals. Now anyone who could get hold of a firearm and who was desperate or committed enough could try his or her hand at commercial robbery. Unfortunately, the introduction of these forms of deskilling and democratisation resulted in a growing number of injuries and fatalities during the 1970s and 1980s. Robberies became increasingly precarious and uncertain encounters in which clerks were often tempted to 'have a go', while the robbers, many of whom were inexperienced in the use of firearms, lived in the fear that enterprising clerks would leap over the counter and grab hold of them or chase them up the street.

A robbery is a robbery is a robbery

To explain something about the motivations of armed robbers we must begin from an appreciation of the specific nature of the offence and, in particular, of the ways in which it is distinguished from other forms of violent and predatory crime. It is useful, therefore, to start from the recognition that one of the distinguishing features of armed robbery is that it crosses the conventional division between violent and property crime and, consequently, it has been counted in both official and academic studies under either or both these headings. The *British Crime Survey*, for example, considers it a form of property crime, while in the *Annual Criminal Statistics* it is identified as a form of violent crime. The fact that armed robbery constitutes only approximately 1 per cent of recorded crime in the UK means such ambiguities have little visible effect on crime reports and crime trends. However, robbery is widely seen as being amongst the most serious of crimes, with approximately 10 per cent of adult males in prison in England and Wales having been convicted of robbery. Thus the analysis of changes in the nature of sentencing and punishment may be significantly affected by these forms of categorisations. Armed robbery can also involve very different levels of force and an array of different weapons. In a percentage of cases, in fact, no weapon is used at all. Thus it should be recognised at the outset that the umbrella term 'armed robbery' is in itself too general a concept to employ as a starting point of analysis and, by the same token, it does not provide a sound basis for analysis or policy formation.

There is also a need to distinguish between forms of armed robbery directed towards commercial targets and those which involve attacks against individuals on the street. Street robbery, or mugging as it is often called, although combined with commercial robberies in the official definition of robbery – the taking of money and goods by the use or threat of force – involves a different victim–offender relation.[1] Significantly, the vast majority of armed robbers whom we interviewed in prison and who had been convicted of robberies against commercial premises expressed disdain and contempt for muggers who targeted vulnerable individuals. Very few of the commercial robbers had any previous involvement in street robbery – despite the fact that, in many cases, they have had an extensive involvement in other forms of crime.

Taking the legal definitions of 'robbery' as the point of departure is, therefore, not only unhelpful but it can also be misleading. A number of potentially useful studies have been undermined by blurring the differences between these two quite different activities (Banton 1985). Forms of investigation that employ an undifferentiated concept of 'robbery' as the basis of analysis have to be treated with extreme caution. In general, it is always a mistake to start the investigation of any from of crime by taking pre-given legal categories as the point of departure. The task of any criminological inquiry is to disaggregate key categories and to explore the relation between their component parts. Such a strategy is important if we are to understand the nature of 'armed' robbery and to identify the forces motivating those robbers who direct their attention towards commercial targets.

A profile of armed robbers

Commercial robbers do not constitute a homogeneous group. The notion that robbers are a specific type of person or that they are all equally dangerous is a fallacy. The research we carried out with commercial robbers in prison revealed vast differences in the types of people who make up this group, particularly in relation to motivation.

To be sure, amongst the 340 convicted robbers we interviewed some general characteristics were evident. The vast majority came from impoverished backgrounds, had a low level of educational achievement and poor work histories. Almost 30 per cent had been in care, where many had begun their criminal careers and had developed an immunity to the pains of institutionalisation, while approximately 20 per cent had been in the army where they had developed a familiarity with firearms. Interestingly, a number of commercial robbers in prison had similar backgrounds to many of the prison wardens who had also been in the army.

Probably the most significant characteristic of this group was that they were overwhelming male. All our prison sample, with one exception, was male. Efforts to try to interview the small number of female armed robbers proved difficult, and the ones who could be tracked down tended either to be accomplices or were not available for an interview. The gender dimension of this group is significant. It says a great deal about motivation and about the social and personal dynamics that underpin this particular form of crime, with its overtones of violence and its association with firearms.

Less than 5 per cent of our prison sample were from ethnic minorities although in the Metropolitan Police sample over 30 per cent were identified as African-Caribbean. Despite the relatively high percentage of commercial robbers in London drawn from the African-Caribbean community the national ethnic minority involvement in commercial robbery stands in contrast to the estimates that some 60 per cent of known street robbers are drawn from this particular ethnic minority group (Hall *et al* 1978; Barker *et al* 1993).

In terms of criminal careers most of our prison sample had histories of involvement in various forms of crime, particularly theft, burglary, drugs and violence, although the extent of involvement varied considerably within the group. There were no clear patterns of offending although approximately 60 per cent of the group had been convicted previously of burglary. The majority were in their twenties at the time they were arrested. Despite certain recurring associations, experiences and characteristics the most remarkable aspect of the prison sample was the diversity of its membership.

Types of armed robbers

Many writers on armed robbery have noted the significant differences within this group in terms of motivation, experience, commitment and the use of firearms. It has become a convention in the literature to divide the population of known commercial robbers into a number of types. Dermott Walsh (1986a), for example, distinguishes between planners and opportunists, while Thomas Gabor and his colleagues (1987) have developed a more elaborate typology dividing robbers into four types – chronic, professional, intensive and occasional. For our purposes, however, we find a threefold division between amateurs, intermediates and professionals to be the most useful.

Amateurs

Contrary to popular opinion, the largest group of known commercial robbers are not the sophisticated career robbers who meticulously plan and execute their crimes but a motley group of amateurs and novices who engage in little planning and often seem unaware of the consequences of their actions. These amateurs are generally characterised by their low level of organisation, their selection of more accessible targets, their lack of experience, their relation to violence and their use of weapons. They will tend to operate alone, they aim for relatively small amounts of money and they have a history of 'failed' or 'attempted' robberies. In many cases the robberies appear as little more than acts of desperation, usually because the person needs money quickly to pay off debts, to buy necessities or to support a drug habit. Two cases exemplify the rather pathetic and inept nature of the criminal activities of members of this group. The first case involves a relatively old offender (aged 60 years) who was interviewed in Parkhurst Prison, and the second involves an 18-year-old offender who was interviewed in Glen Parva Young Offenders Institution.

The older offender (who had white hair and a white beard and who looked a little like Santa Claus) had worked on the pier of a well-known holiday resort for most of his life. In his late fifties he was sacked as a result of the 'rationalisation' of manpower and was unable to find another job. While he was working he had found an imitation handgun, which he had kept and hidden at home. A little while after he was sacked his eldest son (who had a wife and two children) was also made redundant. During an afternoon drinking session in which the father and son attempted to drown their sorrows they decided they would use the replica gun to rob the local building society. Although drunk they went home and got the car and the gun, drove down to the centre of town, parked the car outside the building society, walked in with the imitation firearm, demanded money at the counter and left with a bundle of notes. Unfortunately for them, the building society had a camera outside the premises that picked up the registration number of their car and before the father and son had time to sober up and count the money, they were both arrested. In court the father claimed he was the instigator of the robbery and that it was his gun. He received a four-year sentence while the son was given two years.

At the other end of the age spectrum is an 18-year-old who was interviewed in a young offenders institution near Leicester. He had spent most of his young life in care and had decided to rob a security van. Since leaving care at the age of 16 he had been living with his grandmother. His account of his unsuccessful robbery displayed a remarkable combination of naiveté and incompetence. Having decided on the time and place to rob the security van, he equipped himself with a pair of old overalls that had been issued to him by his previous employer and armed himself with a knife because he felt that, while conveying a threat to the guards it would be less likely to cause serious injury. While the boxes were being unloaded from the security van he threatened one of the guards with the knife, snatched a box and ran off down the road. He took off the overalls and stuffed them into a dustbin and returned to his grandmother's house with the box. He opened it to find it full of shredded computer paper. Unfortunately for him, someone had seen him dispose of the overalls and had alerted the police. The police examined the overalls and found a name neatly stitched at the back of the collar. It only took a day or two for the police to track him down.

Many other cases of desperation and frustration were reported. Four respondents claimed they had carried out the robberies around

Christmas time in order to buy presents for their children, while a number of others claimed they had carried out robberies under pressures from their partners in order to get the money to pay the bills or to feed their family. In many of these cases the robber had been caught as a result of his first robbery. One of the most graphic but not untypical accounts was provided by Martin, who was serving five years in Wormwood Scrubs. He told us that:

> Basically, it was the last straw. I was on the settee at 12 o'clock at night and I could smell the sick and the vomit. I said to the missus 'can you smell it?' She said 'Yeah' and I ran into my little daughter's room and gave her to the missus. She was sick over her. Then the electric went and I didn't have a penny. You know what I mean – not one pence. Couldn't put the electric on. So I stood there with two candles while she was looking after the kid, trying to clean up the vomit and that's when I decided enough is enough. I thought yeah, I'll do it.

The gender dimensions of this case are as significant as the economic circumstances. The robber refused to let his daughter see him in prison and felt it would not be right for her to see him locked up.

Another major constituent of the large group of amateurs were those whose involvement in armed robbery was directly associated with drug use. It is estimated that half the amateurs in the prison sample were under the influence of drugs or alcohol when carrying out the robbery or, alternatively, the robbery was motivated by the desire to purchase drugs. A typical case involved Adam, who was 17 years of age when he was arrested and who was consequently serving a custodial sentence at Stocken Prison. Indicatively, during the robbery he stopped the cashier in the building society from giving him 'too much money':

> *Adam*: Yeah, I actually stopped her giving me the money and grabbed it off her. She was going to give me more.
> *Q*: Why did you stop her?
> *Adam*: I don't know. The adrenaline was going too much. I had to get us moved. I don't really know looking back know, but I suppose I just didn't want to be too greedy really. It looked a lot when it was coming over to start with. I was only young then so it looked all right.
> *Q*: How much were you expecting to get when you went in there?
> *Adam*: Oh I wanted thousands. I thought that I was going to able to settle down for life after that.

Q: How much did you get altogether?
Adam: It was just over £500.

Adam, who was illiterate when he entered prison and who had spent many years in local authority care, is typical of many amateurs in that he had both unrealistic expectations of the amount of money he was likely to get and was unable or unwilling to overcome his anxieties in the building society to maximise his takings. Since being in prison he had taken some basic educational courses and, when asked if he was now able to read and write, he replied with a certain sense of achievement: 'Yeah, I learnt a lot more education wise than I have in all my school outside.'

Many of the accounts of the robberies carried out by the most inexperienced amateurs were conspicuous by the virtual absence of any planning. The amateur robbery is often a response to a particular crisis in the person's uncertain and chaotic life. Paul, for example, who was interviewed in Wormwood Scrubs, decided to rob a building society after loosing a lot of money on the horses and then getting very drunk. He told us:

I was standing you know but I could hardly stand up. I asked for about three grand and she said that she didn't have that type of money. I said I had a gun I my pocket, but I didn't have a gun. I had three fingers, but she thought it was a gun. I told her to put the money in the bag. Then she put in £750 and I thought 'Oh My God,' what am I doing. I've never done a crime like this before in my life. I left the money. I only stole £20. I left the rest of the money on the counter.

Accounts of this type were not uncommon. Many of the robberies committed by these amateurs were unplanned and inept, carried out under the influence of drugs or alcohol with an imitation firearm or pistol and with little or no knowledge of how much money to expect. In many cases the sums stolen were paltry or the robbery was abandoned. In interviews with this group, these amateur robbers repeatedly expressed deep embarrassment at their incompetence and were in some cases reluctant to reveal just how little they had stolen, particularly as they were now doing lengthy prison sentences.

There was one further subgroup amongst the novices and amateurs that approximated to the depiction of 'intensive' robbers suggested by Gabor *et al* (1987). These robbers (although like other amateurs relatively inexperienced and disorganised) were different in that they engaged in a string of armed robberies over a short period of time – either as a self-destruct strategy in which the person, for whatever reason, no longer seemed to care what happened to him, or because of a rapidly spiralling relationship between excessive drug use and armed robbery. Consequently, their engagement in crime was very intense but short lived.

Intermediates

In our prison sample there was a substantive group who were generally more organised and experienced than the amateurs but less dedicated to armed robbery than the professionals. This intermediate group accounted for 25 per cent of the sample. Unlike the amateurs, they engaged in a reasonable level of planning, had long histories of criminal involvement, were more prepared to carry firearms but were less governed by drug use. This group of intermediates divided fairly evenly into two subgroups. On one side there were those who we might refer to as the criminal 'diversifiers' while on the other side were the 'developers' who were in a transitional phase and who saw themselves as becoming more serious and experienced criminals.

The criminal diversifiers involved those whose engagement in armed robbery was sporadic and who mixed robberies with other types of criminal involvement. This group (who tended to be in their late teens or early twenties when imprisoned) admitted to an ongoing involvement in burglary, car theft and drug dealing. Importantly, this group did not identify themselves as armed robbers as such but rather as general-purpose criminals who were prepared to engage in commercial robbery when a suitable opportunity arose. In a number of cases these diversifiers acted on information received or were invited to participate in a robbery planned by others. Some of the respondents in the group expressed the view they were better protected and had less chance of being identified by the police because they moved between different criminal networks. This flexibility, they felt, prevented them from acquiring a criminal profile and it made them more unlikely to be picked up in connection with the investigation of armed robberies (Dorn *et al* 1992).

In one representative case involving a robbery at a public house, one offender was prepared to accept the invitation to participate in armed robbery. He told us:

Well, me and a couple of mates of mine who was really into serious stuff – I was just a burglar – anyway, someone told us there was going to be £15,000 in the safe at the time. For the two guys I was working with it was just a matter of going in there with a gun and taking the money.

Because of the general experience in different types of crime, some of these intermediates were able to decide fairly spontaneously to carry out the robbery when they felt the conditions were right. For example, in one case involving a building society:

This one was not really planned. It was just that we were walking down the street with my mate and we seen it. We went in there and just walked up to the counter and said: 'We would like to make a withdrawal'. She said 'How much?' and we said 'The fucking lot' and she put the money on the counter and we walked out.

This offender reported being involved in a number of other cases and informed us that a robbery would normally involve three or four days' planning. This demonstration of apparent spontaneity and bravado shows a willingness (also expressed by other robbers) to embrace risk and uncertainty and to rely on experience and instinct to pull the robbery off.

The other half of the intermediate group saw themselves not so much as diversifiers but as developers, progressing from minor crimes towards the more serious end of the market. These individuals did not necessarily identify themselves as armed robbers although they may have carried out a number of armed robberies. They did, however, have aspirations to become more professional and to consider more challenging targets.

The promise of joining the 'big time' and progressing from theft and burglaries to targets that are potentially more lucrative was an important motivating factor amongst this group. As one respondent informed us:

We'd been doing burglaries and what not...quite well thought out...and one of my co-defendants said we were only making small money and we could make the big time. 'There's money to be made in this, so let's get ourselves some dosh', he said. I've found a place, a jewellers, it was an antique jewellers and there was £130,000–£140,000 worth of stuff in the window alone. We already had the clothes and everything else we needed. We had the walkie-talkies, we had the overalls, the stocking masks. We used to buy Tesco trainers 'cos if you smash something and you get glass fibres in your shoes or whatever you don't mind throwing away a £5 or £10 pair of trainers rather than your Reeboks.

Despite this commendable frugality he was still a long way away from making it 'big time', and the fact he was caught and given a lengthy prison sentence meant his rate of progression through his criminal career had been temporarily, at least, placed on hold.

Professional and persistent robbers

The level of motivation displayed by the more experienced robbers is distinctly different from that of the other groups. For this smaller rather elite group, robbery was more of a job and a way of life. That is, armed robbery is more directly woven in to the fabric of their daily lives. As Jack Katz (1988) has argued, the decision to become a persistent armed robber is very different from that involved in committing occasional robberies. It involves a commitment to crime and violence and requires a conception of oneself as a career robber and a villain. An inquiry into the motives associated with this group becomes, therefore, a question of understanding what makes robbery attractive over time. It is not only a matter of identifying external pressures or psychological predispositions but also of identifying the meanings individuals attach to robbery that make it an appropriate kind of illicit activity to pursue. For the most part a long-term commitment to serious crimes such as robbery involves a contempt for conventional lifestyles. It involves not only the embracing of risk but also its realisation. Not surprisingly, there is considerable interest amongst the members of this group in different forms of gambling.

The main differences between persistent robbers and the other groups is in the level of planning, selection of targets, the use of firearms and the deployment of violence. Typically, professionals will work with known associates and spend weeks rather than days planning a robbery. Operating in groups of three or four rather than one or two professionals requires the use of a much more elaborate range of equipment and will normally involve more than one vehicle for each job. Escape routes will be carefully mapped out since the consequences of getting caught are known to be serious. For the same reason they tend to aim for more lucrative targets and are prepared to take on unusual targets if they promise rich rewards.

One example of such a target involved an attack at a race track in which the robbers broke into the ticket office just after the race meeting had started. This was an experienced team of armed robbers who had carefully planned and co-ordinated the robbery. They purchased unmarked weapons and stole three or four cars, which were strategically placed for the getaway. Gloves, balaclavas and overalls were all worn during the robbery and later burned in the back of the car while they made their escape. Loaded shotguns and handcuffs were used and the robbers got away with approximately £37,000. Some of them were caught later as a result of a police surveillance operation. The member of the team who was interviewed was asked why they decided to rob the race track. He replied with an air of despondency that there are now very few place that carry large amounts of cash which are not heavily protected. Thus the race track appeared to be a relatively vulnerable and attractive target, although after deducting 'expenses' each of the four robbers involved took approximately £7,000 each for this high-risk and high-profile robbery.

For the persistent armed robber violence has to become part of one's persona. Many of the professional armed robbers we interviewed took great pride in their ability to instil instant fear into security guards and cashiers. In order to commit oneself to robbery one must readily display a commitment to violence. To scare guards and cashiers and to maintain a reputation as a serious villain, it is necessary to be able to resort quickly and convincingly to violence. One way of achieving this objective is to give a prior demonstration of one's violent capabilities by engaging in apparently gratuitous or 'irrational' violence at the onset of the robbery. By the same token, carrying loaded firearms is an essential part of one's repertoire of violence.

Many of these more experienced villains are known to each other and tend to drink in the same establishments. Certain areas of the inner city – invariably deprived and run-down areas – become associated with serious crimes such as armed robbery. As one interviewee from London told us:

Now, when you got an area like Bermondsey and Deptford, you got heavy villains. Now everyone looks at these 'faces'. Everyone aspires to be like them. So, therefore, from a very early age you got this built-in criminal pecking order of which you want to be a part. So obviously you progress through life. You might start off with a bit of theft. Then it's a bit of taking and driving away, then it's a bit of burglary, then it's a robbery, then it's armed robbery and before you know it you're a wheel.

The association with the high life and 'easy money' stands in stark contrast to the poverty and sense of hopelessness rife in such areas. Clearly for some the prospect of having cash in their pockets and drinking with the 'boys' and the 'faces' was more attractive, whatever the risk and the penalty, than a life of drudgery. It is important to be 'seen', to be engaging in conspicuous consumption, to be having fun and not to care. This is an important masculinist mark of success (Lyng 1990; Collinson 1996).

Thus it is clear there are considerable differences in the backgrounds and motivation of these three groups of robbers. It would be possible to draw up a detailed typology differentiating these groups in relation to planning, choice of targets, average amounts stolen, range of equipment used and the deployment of weapons and violence. However, although the distinctions between these groups are not always clear cut the failure to take into account such differences will result in the production of essentialising stereotypes, unrealistic policies and a limited appreciation of the ways in which motivation is structured amongst different groups of people. It should also be noted that motivations can change over time. Younger robbers, for example, were likely to be motivated by peer group pressure and the excitement of carrying out such a daring crime. But as robbers grow older there appears to be a gradual shift towards financial need and the desire for 'high living' (Cook 1991).

Taking this typology as our point of reference, a number of themes emerged in the course of the research that appeared to influence the dynamics of armed robbery and to impact more or less directly on the issues of motivation. These themes include media, money, drugs, violence and rationality.

The influence of the media

There has been considerable controversy over the relation between the media and involvement and attitudes towards crime and violence. There is no space here to try to resolve these long-standing disputes but some comments on the role of the media in stimulating motivation do seem in order. Suffice it is to say that while it is difficult to believe the media does not have some effect on people's orientation towards crime and violence it is not the case that the media systematically turns otherwise law-abiding individuals into hardened criminals but, rather, performs a sensitising role that instructs or encourages those already predisposed to crime and violence to express these tendencies (Hall *et al* 1978; Sparks 1992).

Much of the classic material that has explored the relationship between the media and crime has come to the conclusion the media tend to dramatise events and to present the atypical as typical (Young 1971). The 'mass' nature of the media means they tend to present a generally undifferentiated picture of armed robbers. Consequently, all armed robbers are depicted as being equally 'dangerous', and films and books conspicuously focus on the more dramatic and daring robberies, presenting robbers as either vicious psychopaths or as cold, calculating criminals. As we have suggested, the vast majority of armed robbers we interviewed did not approximate to either of these images and, instead, appeared as largely desperate and disorganised and, in some cases, as sadly pathetic and inept.

Our sample of armed robbers in prison were asked specifically to comment on media influences. One respondent felt the media affected the police and the courts. He claimed: 'The police latch on to cases that catch the public's eye, and obviously the more attention the case gets the more bird – nine times out of ten – you're going to get.' A number of others made reference to programmes like *The Sweeney* and *The Bill* which, they said, had alerted them to the possibilities of armed robbery while conveying the message the police are fairly ineffective in dealing with crimes of this type. Some referred to films and programmes they had seen on television that had shown armed robbers who had carried out robberies with style and without being caught. A percentage of the robbers who were interviewed clearly identified with these characters and were able to remember in considerable detail the films and programmes they had seen and the ways in which the robberies were carried out.

For some robbers the influence of the media was less to do with depictions of crime and violence and more to do with a general message about social relations. As one respondent put it: 'I'll tell you what the media does. The media makes you want to go out and take what you want yourself, because they let you know that nobody else in the country gives a damn about you.' For others there were clear indications the media presented appealing images of 'the good life' in which the division between wants and needs was blurred. The media conveyed the message that, if they did not fully participate in consumption, they were missing out. Robbery provided one way of fulfilling these aspirations.

What was noticeable, however, was the number of robbers who found it difficult to recall or name a film that had influenced them. Most of their influences and role models were drawn from the street and from the networks of associates with whom they came into contact. One exception to this was *Crimewatch UK* and similar types of programmes. These programmes, which are designed to catch robbers, performed a different function for the robbers in prison. They provide a source of information, interest and amusement. As one robber informed us:

Crimestoppers. I watch it just in case I sort of recognise someone I might know out on the streets . . . Crimewatch UK is always a good thing to watch 'cos you can always find different bits of information, what sort of, like, new materials they are using and things like that.

Another robber expressed the view that: 'They reckon Crimewatch ties up cases, yeah, but they actually show you how the crime is done and that's what gives people ideas in their head, like, if they can do it, I can do it.' Another reported: 'It was Crimewatch that gave us the idea of how to carry out the robberies that I am now serving a sentence for.' Similarly: 'I saw some robberies on Crimewatch. They seemed really easy. Just whack the gun on the till and they give you the money. It seemed so easy.'

Comments of this type were expressed by a significant number of our group of convicted robbers and there was little doubt that *Crimewatch UK* was the most popular television programme in prison. It provides a regular update of changing techniques and innovations while providing a source of new ideas. It provides a chance for robbers and other criminals to see if any of their friends and acquaintances are featured and, above all, it provides some degree of comfort to those incarcerated robbers to know that, despite the fact the robbers have been caught on video, they are still at large.

Money, money, money

Among the main objectives of any armed robbery is the acquisition of money, preferably in the form of cash. But the money has a number of different meanings and uses amongst different types of robbers. For many of the amateurs, money provided the means to buy essentials, to pay of debts or to finance a drug habit. Alternatively, as we have seen, amongst the intermediate group the takings from robberies were used to finance both legitimate and illegitimate business activities as well as to deal in drugs or other commodities.

For other young aspiring robbers, the aim is to 'earn it and burn it'. Money is not for saving or investing but for spending. As one young robber was happy to let us know: 'Yeah, exactly, we won't see each other until we've spent our money and it will be gone in days – a couple of days. Say £5,000 will be gone in a week at the most. Two and a half grand each. It's gone.' Not surprisingly, although some of these robbers were carrying out robberies on a fairly regular basis, they reported they were continuously broke. When asked what they spent their money on, many mentioned luxury goods:

I spent it on jewellery, bought some clothes, got my hair cut to change my appearance...I spent it on meals taking my girlfriends out, buying toys for my baby to be born. Silly things like that 'cos it's not your own and you can spend it double quick...When it's from a bank and you've got it in your pocket, its like burning a hole in your pocket.

Amongst the more professional robbers money has a somewhat different significance. The amount of money taken is a mark of status and is required to take care of the economic pressures and to support an appropriate lifestyle. However, some of the money taken will be reinvested in other enterprises – particularly drug dealing.

Whether buying necessities, paying off debts, supporting dependants, scoring drugs, purchasing luxury goods or using the money to live the high life, the reality is the amount of money taken from all commercial robberies is surprisingly low and there is a good percentage of robberies in which no money is taken or which for some reason are aborted. Alternatively, the robbers are caught before they have a chance to spend the money. As might be expected, the inexperienced amateurs tend to have the highest 'failure' rate and engage in robberies in which sums involved are embarrassingly low; the intermediate group, on the other hand, will tend to be more successful because of better planning and greater experience and will normally take between £2,000 and £10,000 on a successful robbery. The professionals will aim higher and go for more lucrative targets and will occasionally hit the 'big one'. But since they have more expenses and larger 'teams', the takings per robber are not excessive.

Drugs

Reference to drugs normally took one of two forms – either in relation to drug taking or drug dealing – although there was often an overlap between these two activities. In terms of drug taking, there appear to be two basic scenarios. The first is that the person takes the drugs or consumes the alcohol and then decides to carry out a robbery. The second is they decide to do a robbery and then take drugs or consume a quantity of alcohol to help them go through with it. Indicatively, Robert (who was interviewed in Grendon Prison) said:

We did a robbery. I took two acid tabs, a couple of temazepan, downers, drunk a couple of cans of special brew, and I had some coke as well, but that was just a everyday thing you know. It makes you feel super-human. You feel really positive about going in and doing it. No one can stop you. You know you're doing it.

Whereas Robert felt the cocktail of drugs put him in control, others reported that being under the influence of drugs – particularly cocaine – made them paranoid and violent. Another convicted robber, Jason, whom we interviewed in Grendon Prison and who had robbed an off-licence with a loaded Smith and Wesson, said: 'Cocaine brought out the beast in me. I lost all sense of responsibility. All sense of caring. I became very violent. I suffered a personality change. I was able to do things that I would not normally do.'

Both Jason and Robert admitted supporting their drug taking though crime. Jason was spending in the region of £1,000 a week at that time on cocaine. However, it would be erroneous on the basis of these admissions to propose a direct causal link between drug taking and crime. A number of people we interviewed were involved in regular drug use but avoided taking drugs prior to a robbery, particularly the more professional robbers who clearly saw drug taking and crime as relatively unrelated activities. As one young robber who was at Glen Parva Young Offenders Institution told us: 'I take drugs and do crime, but if I didn't take drugs I would still do the crime and vice versa.' The relation between drug taking and crime in this and other cases is not necessarily causal, and where there are causal links they may not be in the expected direction. That is, it may well be that criminal involvement precedes the drug taking by a significant period of time. For many of the prisoners we interviewed, the relation between drugs and crime was less direct, formed part of a general lifestyle and was bound up with a complex matrix of social relations and social attitudes in which drugs may well have an 'elective affinity' to crime rather than a direct causal connection (Mackenzie and Uchida 1994; Matthews and Trickey 1995). As Robert indicated, drug taking was perceived by many respondents as a normal activity and as a regular feature of a certain lifestyle. The taking of drugs both enhanced and mediated the risk associated with armed robbery.

Amongst the more organised and professional robbers, the interest in drugs was mainly in relation to drug dealing and the proceeds from robberies were reported to be regularly reinvested in illicit drugs. On some occasions a robbery might be arranged for the specific purpose of financing a drug deal. Derek, who was interviewed in Swaleside Prison, stated: 'Yeah, most money, particularly where I come from in London got illegally from armed robberies will wind up in some sort of drugs deal... If you want to turn some money over and get a good profit the only obvious thing nowadays is drugs.' This view was endorsed by many of the professional armed robbers we interviewed who explained that, by reinvesting the proceeds from an armed robbery into a drugs deal, they could expect to double their money. In some interviews it was reported that the bigger drug dealers themselves sometimes became the object of armed raids since they were known to hold significant amounts of cash and were unable to rely on police protection. One older robber (who had grown up in east London) told us rather nostalgically that the greater involvement of armed robbers in drug dealing had made people more suspicious of each other and that rather than just going out and spending all the proceeds of the robbery and having a good time, now the money was continually reinvested such that: 'People aren't so sociable. They're more paranoid, you know, and whereas you used to have big family get-togethers ... It doesn't happen anymore. Everyone is suspicious and wary of each other with this drug business.'

Violence

The differential commitment to violence amongst the prison sample became abundantly clear. Many of those located at the amateur and inexperienced end of the continuum displayed considerable reservations about the use of any kinds of violence. Interviews with this group of robbers were replete of incidents where they waited for the shop or the post office to empty of customers in order to minimise the risk to bystanders. In many of these cases robbers carried replica guns or no gun at all and, if confronted with refusal or non-cooperation by counter staff, they hastily retreated. This may help to explain the relatively low rate of injuries suffered by the victims of commercial robberies (Morrison and O'Donnell 1994).

At the other end of the spectrum was a percentage of robbers who carried loaded firearms and who were prepared to use violence at the least provocation. In fact, in some cases robbers engaged in what might appear as gratuitous or 'irrational' forms of violence in order to impose control, enforce compliance and minimise the possibility of victim resistance. Cashiers, bystanders or security staff who 'had a go' were seen generally as being 'responsible' for any violence that might be directed towards them. Around half the robbers interviewed admitted they were prepared to use violence when people 'had a go' or refused to co-operate. Such an act was seen by the robbers as stupid and irrational since it was not their money and, therefore, there was no justification for their intervention.

For many the initial aim of the robbery is to gain control. In their accounts of carrying out robberies the term 'control' featured frequently. The imposition of control clearly went beyond the pragmatic considerations of limiting victim resistance. It was bound up with the expression of power and with the 'buzz' of the adrenaline rush that went with it. The graphic terms in which this experience was reported and the level of animation that accompanied these accounts signified the importance of the process of taking control. As one robber succinctly put it: 'The most important thing is I've got to get control.'

In the words of another robber:

As soon as I get on the bus...and from that very moment I'm in a trance-like state. No matter what happens between then and going into the building society. I don't really take account of anything 'cos my mind is so fixed on what's happening. I am also very conscious of instilling a sense of fear into the teller behind the desk, by the look in my eyes, my clenched teeth, absolute eye contact with them.

The overlap between the 'buzz' experienced in the armed robbery and that which is associated with drug use was often referred to:

It's just like when you do coke, you get a rush out of it, but when you've got a gun in your hands, people are listening to you. They're doing as they are told. You're in full control. It's just brilliant. You're just there. You're the man. You're like God.

The desire to take control and to exercise power in this way clearly has its own attractions, apart from the money. In lives that are disorganised and chaotic this moment of control provides a semblance of order while simultaneously producing an adrenaline rush, which a number of robbers reported as being addictive. Some robbers admitted they sometimes engaged in robberies even if they did not desperately need the money because they missed the excitement (Jammers 1995).

Andrew, an intermediate diversifier from Liverpool, said:

Always high, always on a high like, get off on doing the buzz, the buzz of actually doing the whatever like, job, 'cos we do burglaries as well, like, get off on that get off on whatever. To actually do a job and walk out of a sort of like bank, post office, when you got sort of like twenty or thirty grand, you can't get a better buzz than that.

It should be noted that even those who were quite clearly prepared to use violence in the course of the robbery and to shoot cashiers and police if they deemed it necessary tended to distance themselves from other forms of violence, particularly that directed towards women and children. Even for hardened armed robbers people who practised such forms of violence were beneath contempt. Thus it was evident that the expression of violence is primarily relational rather than purely situational, as rational choice theorists claim (Shoham 1997). As Colin from Swaleside Prison pointed out: 'Yeah, I am a violent man. I know I'm a violent man, but only within a specific sphere. I am not violent to everybody.' When asked about domestic violence he replied: 'I think, it's very sad. If two people can't live together without bashing each other up every day then they should find different partners', while in relation to children he emphasised that: 'I deplore any violence against children...I've got nine children and I've never beaten any of my children'. In sum, the use of violence is often selective and instrumental. As opposed to the popular depiction of violence as being 'out of control', the violence expressed by the armed robber often involves taking and exercising control (Stanko 2000).

The rational robber?

In some of the recent literature on armed robbery, robbers have been depicted as rational agents operating according to utilitarian cost-benefit calculus (Feeney and Weir 1986). Employing varieties of rational choice theory, these writers have identified the decision to engage in robbery, the selection of the targets and the carrying out the robbery as an expression of a rational decision-making process on the part of the robber. Such an approach is, however, crude and simplistic and reduces a complex process of motivation into an unrealistic dichotomy of rational/irrational action (see Walsh 1986b; Wright and Bennett 1994).

As noted above, a significant number of the robbers who were interviewed were drunk or on drugs immediately prior to the robbery or during it. In a large percentage of cases the robbers were desperate and were driven either by the need to find money urgently to feed and clothe their families or, alternatively, to finance a drug habit. The fact that in many cases robbers have little or no idea how much money is available and only a limited awareness of the security measures in place makes any suggestion of a rational cost-benefit analysis taking place in the minds of the majority of robbers unrealistic.

The gratuitous use of excessive violence as a consequence of poor planning or limited co-operation on the part of cashiers or bystanders can hardly be seen as a strategy for maximising rewards and minimising punishments. Wrapped up in these demonstrations of violence are forms of machismo and bravado that are tied to the desire to control and dominate, however shortlived the experience may be (Messerscmidt 1993; Bourgois 1996).

Probably the most difficult aspect of armed robbery for rational choice theory to explain is the active pursuit of risk and danger. The pursuit of risk, which becomes the trademark of the experienced professional robber, does not fit well into the notion of the armed robber as a rational actor. In fact, the rational/irrational dichotomy makes little sense in this context. There can be no doubt that robbers employ contingent rationalities and make decisions based on certain knowledge, experience and hunches. However, these contingent rationalities need to be understood in a complex and contradictory framework of motivations and values, which in turn are conditioned by a culturally generated set of attitudes and social relations and which themselves embody contradictory and inconsistent elements.

Instead of exploring these complex processes rational choice theory adopts the notion of 'rationality' both as an assumption and as an explanation. Clearly, as Cornish and Clarke (1986) note, 'Retrospective accounts may fail to capture the essential elements of real-life decision-making' and, by implication, tend to impose a fictional rationality on a range of diverse and contradictory processes. The distinction between 'bounded' and 'perfect' rationality does not overcome these problems. The majority of robbers do not carefully weigh up costs and benefits and take into consideration the relevant factors. Instead they tend to be governed by immediate pressures, changing moods, impressions and the search for excitement, and are often fuelled by alcohol and drugs. The majority of robbers we interviewed did not really think about being caught, and they were generally unaware of what kind of sentence they would receive if they did get caught.

Significantly, rational choice theory is unable to say anything very interesting about the cognitive process involved in engaging in crime in general and in armed robbery in particular. It is therefore forced to 'import' a mix of psychological explanations in order to try to fill this gap. The plausibility of these explanations is extremely questionable. These 'imported' psychological accounts, however, throw little light on the meaning of 'rationality' and therefore they have little real explanatory value. Thus, as Barry Hindess (1988) has argued, the main problem with rational choice theory is that 'It obscures important questions of techniques, procedures, forms of thought, employed by different actors'.

A similar criticism can be laid at the door of the routine activities approach, which claims that for a crime to occur there needs to be an attractive target, a likely offender and the absence of capable guardians (Cohen and Felson 1979). What constitutes an 'attractive' target involves a highly subjective and often idiosyncratic judgement while, as we have seen, many convicted robbers are amongst the most unlikely suspects (Ekblom and Tilley 2000). Private security companies and most other commercial organisations that handle money employ a considerable number of capable guardians and therefore as a way of trying to explain armed robbery and similar crimes, routine activities theory is woefully inadequate. But most importantly for our purposes routine activity theory takes offender motivation as a constant and therefore fails to provide the basis for analysing this important dimension of the process.

An incisive critique of rational choice theory as applied to robbery has been provided by Jack Katz (1988), who has argued in relation to persistent robbers that it makes little sense to see their involvement in robbery, their commitment to violence and their involvement in drugs and gambling as a series of rational acts. Moreover, as we have indicated, the group Katz examines could be considered to be most 'rational', and the majority of the non-professional robbers employ an even lower level of 'rationality'. In criticising the voluntarism of rational choice theory, however, Katz presents his own version of 'voluntarism' when he writes 'My overall objective in this book is to demonstrate that the causes of crime are constructed by the offenders themselves'. Thus rather than seeing poverty, deprivation, poor education, unemployment, cultural norms and gender relations as being amongst the determinants of armed robbery, he attempts to claim these conditions are the product of individual aspirations and of free floating will.

Moralities and motivation

The decision to engage in a serious crime like armed robbery, however desperate and overdetermined particular individuals may feel, always involves engaging in moral choices. It involves not only a response to the pressures and inducements that may propel people towards various forms of crime but also the ability to overcome certain moral constraints.

For some of the more experienced and committed robbers the moral constraints on committing armed robberies were in part overcome by the employment of techniques of neutralisation – it's not their money, no one will miss the money, they are insured, banks exploit people anyway. Similarly, the use of violence is rationalised by the claim 'they asked for it' or that 'they get paid to work in banks or building societies and they know the risks'. A succinct summary of the techniques was provided by the Italian armed robber who pulled off the famous Knightsbridge safety deposit box robbery in 1987.[2] With reference to banks he claims;

I mean they exploit people. They never lend you *their* money. They lend you *my* money. I think that the Nat West profit was something like £1 bn, something like that. Now to me its too easy to say it's some sort of redistribution process, but I mean let's put it this way. I don't have a pension, I don't have any clients' money. They are insured so I am taking out money that will be replaced anyway, so you know, I can't see any immoral business in there. An illegal one yes, of course, but I think it is the least of all crimes. Well it's a dangerous situation where people can get hurt, but then you can get hurt just walking your dog or being killed by psychopaths and these perverts who are knocking around (Viccei 1992).

As this quotation indicates, some robbers make a distinction between immoral and illegal actions. It was also the case that different illegal actions were associated with different forms of morality. The condemnation of sex offenders, child molesters and other 'scum' allows many robbers to claim a few square feet of the moral high ground and to contrast their actions with those of 'perverts' and 'nonces', despite their apparent willingness to resort to violence. Armed robbers, no more or less than other groups of offenders, are not amoral calculators. Indeed, many of those who were interviewed express regret, remorse and, in some cases, guilt and shame (Wortley 1996). The whole issue of crime is infused with issues of morality, guilt and struggles over identity and recognition (Honneth 1995). If it were only about stealing goods or money it would be of considerably less social interest.

While in prison some offenders openly express remorse and see their actions as unjustifiable and stupid. There were reports of benefits from attending the Violence Reduction Programmes offered in prison. For some, no doubt, prison life represented a 'school of crime' in which they learned more about unlawful activities and developed criminal contacts. However, prison for some provided a kind of sanctuary and gave offenders the opportunity to reflect on their actions and lives and led a number to decide either because of moral concerns (it was wrong), pragmatic considerations (that it did not produce reasonable rewards) or because of age (too old to do another long prison sentence) to desist from armed robbery in the future.

Conclusion

Armed robbery is an offence that commands a unique position in the trajectory of crime. It is replete with ambiguities and complexities. It attracts both acclamation and contempt. In its more dramatic forms it attracts media and public attention, whilst in its more mundane forms it is virtually ignored by both the general public and academic researchers. It is widely seen as a form of crime that is glamorous, lucrative and highly specialist. In reality much armed robbery is a desperate and routine activity.

There is enormous variation in the circumstances that draw different individuals into armed robbery as well as very different levels of involvement. Like much previous research we have developed a basic typology in order to distinguish between the different types of armed robbers we interviewed. This typology suggests that, in relation to criminal careers, planning, choice of target, amount of money sought and stolen, and the use of weapons that our sample can be divided into three fairly distinct groups. Such a differentiation, we believe, is a necessary starting point for the analysis of commercial robbery and for the development of policy responses. As in other studies we found that the amateurs and novices had a relatively low level of planning, poor disguises, a tendency to use imitation firearms or other weapons, to have carried out fewer robberies and to be more likely to attack more accessible and vulnerable targets; while experiencing a high rate of failure (Koppen and Jansen 1998).

The intermediate group were a more mixed group, combining those who had more extensive levels of criminal involvement and more experience of robberies. In general, they engaged in more planning, used better disguises, carried firearms (although not always real or loaded) and were prepared to attack more difficult targets. Professional robbers, in contrast, planned carefully, wore more elaborate disguises, used loaded firearms and were more committed to the success of the robbery, even if it involved using excessive force.

In opposition to the conception of the armed robber as a rational actor as portrayed in rational choice theory, we have suggested that the range of decision-making which offenders like armed robbers engage in cannot be usefully mapped out in relation to a rational/irrational dichotomy. Many of the leading propositions associated with rational choice theory are untestable and tautological and are not open to empirical verification or refutation (Opp 1997). Although rational choice theory comes in a number of different forms associated with different concepts of 'rationality', it is the case that it offers a form of explanation that throws little light on the generic causal mechanisms which shape the involvement of different types of actors in offences such as armed robbery. We have noted that the vast majority of those convicted of armed robbery come from poor neighbourhoods, have low educational achievements and a significant percentage have been in care. The levels of personal disorganisation and desperation expressed by many of these robbers – particularly the amateurs – together with the absence of planning and lack of awareness of security systems mean that, in reality, their chances of pulling off a successful armed robbery are always going to be minimal. For some of the more experienced robbers, robbery did not so much represent the outcome of a process of cost-benefit decision-making but, rather, provided a way of embracing risk and danger. It also represented the expression of highly gendered modalities of power and control in a world that was, for many, highly chaotic and uncertain.

Notes

1 Studies of street robbery indicate that muggers tend to be concentrated in the 16–19 years age group and that, in London, it appears to be associated with young people of African-Caribbean origin (Burney 1990; Barker et al 1993).
2 In the interview, Valerio Viccei pointed out that not one of the owners of the safety deposit boxes in Knightsbridge actually came forward to reclaim his or her possessions after the robbery. He said that in these boxes he had found among other things large quantities of cocaine and collections of jewellery worth hundreds of thousands of pounds.

Chapter 3

Doing the business

Introduction

In principle, carrying out an commercial armed robbery is a relatively straightforward exercise. It simply involves selecting an appropriate target, walking into the premises, threatening the cashier with a real or implied weapon, demanding the money, putting the money in a bag and walking out. However, in practice, the variations on this model are endless and the constraints and controls that are now in place in most commercial establishments create a number of potential complications and difficulties. The general impediments to carrying out a successful robbery include victim resistance and the presence of a range of security devices, as well as a number of unforeseen and unforeseeable contingencies. In one robbery, for example, in which the robber's co-defendant 'lost his bottle' on the way in to the bank, the robber who was interviewed decided the best way to proceed with robbing these premises – which he had unsuccessfully tried to rob on a previous occasion – was to take a customer hostage:

I went in there and as I walked in I grabbed an African woman – a Nigerian woman. The teller shut his window. This Pakistani teller and the African... couldn't understand each other. As I grabbed the customer, her wig and hair net came off and another bloke – a South African – was trying to attack me... It's all on camera, but I don't remember hitting the customer. This is on camera – me hitting the customer – he's got two stitches. I grabbed the woman... I'm trying to calm her down. The teller's window was shut and the manager's come out of the back and said: 'I know you from last time,' and it all went off so quick. He was fighting me so I had to smash the window of the door, 'cos I pushed the door instead of pulling it...And I'm panicking now and I'm starting to lose all my marbles, you know, so I smashed the windows trying to get out and people are looking in from the outside now you see...So I pulled the door and escaped, and as I was saying, that's all I remember. Getting in the car I was so shaken that my mate said: 'What's that in your hand?' and I said it looks like a wig or something...

Even some of the experienced armed robbers made reference to the danger of unanticipated problems arising in the course of the robbery, despite considerable planning and expertise. As one professional armed robber, who specialised in robbing security vans, put it:

You do everything right and nine times out of ten you get the money, but there's always that one in ten that you don't. On one we got the guard out and threatened to blow his legs off. The driver just wouldn't have none of it. Just a cool bastard. Didn't give a crap about his mate, and if we'd shot him I don't think that he would have done nothing. He just wouldn't give the money.

A number of robbers reported being bewildered in situations where rising screens had isolated them on the wrong side of the counter or in cases in which the counter staff disappeared from view or refused to co-operate. In several cases robbers reported arriving five or ten minutes after the tills had been cleared. There were two cases in which the police were already present when the robbers arrived to carry out a robbery, and a further two cases in which robbers accidentally rammed into the police while making their getaway. In one case a potentially successful robbery was foiled because the getaway car driver decided to speed up and drive erratically when seeing a police patrol car. In one more bizarre case a young man robbed a local arcade where he knew the female attendant and, when she refused to co-operate, he stabbed her a number of times. She later identified him as the robber and he was arrested. Numerous other examples could be given of bad luck or bad judgement on the part of robbers but what was remarkable from the cases that were examined was how such an apparently straightforward crime could so frequently go wrong.

Some cases, however, did reflect a semblance of ingenuity and imagination, such as the robber who pretended to be blind and who carried a white stick in order to surprise the guards in a security van; or the robber who used a wheelchair to rob a supermarket, concealing a shotgun beneath a blanket that was spread across his lap. In one reported robbery that took place in Surrey, a security van was trapped between two vehicles while the main road was blocked by another vehicle. While all the vehicles were stationary one of the robbers went along all the cars taking their ignition keys. This in turn created a traffic jam that prevented the police from reaching the scene of the crime. The team of robbers got away with half a million pounds.

Recent trends in armed robbery

Despite the shortcomings of even the most experienced armed robbers, as well as the widespread adoption of security measures by commercial organisations, the number of armed robberies recorded in England and Wales against commercial premises increased steadily during the 1980s reaching a peak in 1993–94, after which there was a sudden downturn. The most frequent target of armed robberies in this period was shops, followed by building societies. Although the overall trend amongst different commercial targets was similar in this period (see Figure 3.1), there were some significant variations in the scale and timing of increases between the different targets with attacks, for example, against building societies peaking much earlier and declining significantly after 1991. After 1994 the number of attacks decreased for all targets, with building societies experiencing a 46 per cent decrease while banks experienced a 43 per cent decrease between 1994 and 1995. At the same time the number of attacks against post offices and garages increased by 12 per cent and 13 per cent, respectively.

Amongst the smaller retail outlets – shops, off-licences, garages and the like – it was estimated in the report on *Crime Against Small Business* (Wood *et al* 1996) that 7.7 per cent of such outlets experienced a robbery over a period of a year and that over half these were attempts. These robberies were not evenly distributed, but tended to be concentrated in particular areas and some businesses were found to be repeatedly victimised (Wood *et al* 1996).

These variations and countervailing trends suggest that the overall volume of armed robbery is conditioned by extraneous social and economic forces as well as by changing forms of motivation, combined with the different forms of security that have been put in place in different types of premises to deter or deflect robbers. Within these constraints a key factor is the criteria employed by prospective robbers in selecting an appropriate target.

Figure 3.1: Robbery offences recorded by the police in which firearms were reported to have been used (by location of offence, England and Wales 1985–95).

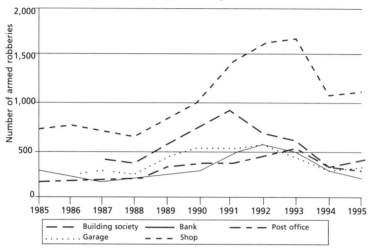

Source: Home Office (1996a)

Selecting targets

The process by which robbers select targets is not quite an art and even less a science. Different people we interviewed identified different considerations. Many of these considerations were blindingly obvious (e.g. not to rob premises near police stations) or the result of undigested wisdom (e.g. not to carry out robberies on certain days of the week). Indicatively, few had a comprehensive set of criteria and were usually guided by one or two basic propositions. There were a number of cases in which people, having outlined certain key criteria that, they maintained, normally guided them towards the selection of a particular target, admitted they had not actually employed these criteria in recent jobs they had carried out. The selection of 'suitable' targets was in many cases based upon a kind of criminal folklore that was dependent, in turn, on a hotchpotch of commonsense notions mixed with popular anecdotes. A considerable degree of fatalism was also expressed, with targets being selected or deselected on the basis of hunches, intuitions or omens of good or bad luck.

A good example of this reliance on hunches and intuition was the timing of the robbery. Amongst those interviewed, different rationalisations and hypothesis were given to justify the time of day at which the robbery was carried out. For some, first thing in the morning was preferred since it was believed this would be the time when there would be the most money on the premises, either because it was assumed organisations stock up with fresh money each morning or because it was believed cash tends to be deposited towards the end of the working day so that each morning there would be a considerable amount of cash available. Others felt the end of the day was the best time because deposits would be made regularly during the day and because organisations were likely to 'cash up' each night and remove any surplus from the premises. In the same way, some opted for the beginning of week and others robberies were conducted when it 'felt right' and there was little awareness of when the most advantageous time to carry out the robbery may be. In a significant number of cases it was reported that the robbery had been carried out just after large amounts of cash had been removed from the premises. This claim, however, may in some cases have been a rationalisation designed to cover ineptitude, lack of planning and poor takings.

Among the criteria that were identified in the course of the interviews with commercial robbers in prisons, there appeared to be a loose trade-off between the amount of money identified as being available and the accessibility and perceived vulnerability of the target. This, however, was not exactly a trade-off between costs and benefits because, as became evident when we explored these criteria in more detail, the conceptions robbers had of the amounts available and the assessments that were made of accessibility and vulnerability were often wildly inaccurate.

Amounts of money available

Different types of robbers had very different expectations of what to expect from a robbery. For some, a hundred pounds was considered a reasonable amount while, at the other end of the spectrum, the objective was hundreds of thousands of pounds and the possibility of 'the big one'. In reality most robbers had only a vague idea of what to expect. Sometimes they were pleasantly surprised but most of the time they were bitterly disappointed.

When targets were selected with little or no planning the amount of money available was largely a matter of luck. However, even amongst the more professional and organised robbers there was a considerable amount of guesswork because different commercial organisations have learned to remove cash from the premises on a regular basis, to vary the amounts held at any one time and to distribute the cash around the premises so that only limited amounts are available at any particular time in any location.

Table 3.1: Amount stolen in the Metropolitan Police Department and South Yorkshire (by target).

| | MPD | | South Yorkshire | |
	No. of cases	Average take (£)	No. of cases	Average take (£)
Bank	54	3,285	11	4,624
Building society	43	7,956	21	1,673
Post office	30	9,732	21	3,990
Cash-in-transit	28	51,445	0	0
Betting shop	71	1,141	6	910
Jewellers	9	206,427	0	0

A review of the cases examined in London between in 1994 and 1995 and in South Yorkshire in 1993 reveals there are considerable differences in the average takings from different types of target. As Table 3.1 indicates, the takings from security vehicles tend to be far greater than that available from such commercial institutions as banks, building societies, betting shops, off-licenses and post offices. Although these figures include attempted robberies in which nothing was stolen, it should be noted that both the reported averages for cash-in-transit and for jewellers are inflated in the Metropolitan Police Department (MPD) as a result of the inclusion of one cash-in-transit robbery of £2.3 million and a jewellery robbery where the takings were an estimated £3 million. Similarly, the figures for South Yorkshire for post offices are inflated by one robbery that netted almost £1 million. In South Yorkshire there were a considerable number of robberies from shops, garages and off-licenses that were dealt with by the Criminal Intelligence Department. Indicatively, the average takings from shops were £355, from garages £310 and off-licenses £79.

The number of robberies that were unsuccessful was instructive. In South Yorkshire almost one in three armed robberies were unsuccessful. In post offices and shops the ratio rose to one in two. In London the number of armed robberies in which nothing was stolen was considerably less, at around 10 per cent for Band 1 robberies. However, there were over 30 cases in which the takings were less than £500, and the vast majority of this group (who were eventually caught) never got to spend any of the money they stole.

Accessibility

The location of the premises was an important consideration for a number of robbers, both in terms of access and the possibility of escape.

Most who commented on locations preferred premises that were situated in a relatively busy area but that could be surveyed for a while before the robbery. There was an even split amongst the robbers interviewed over the question of the perceived benefits of the inside of the premises being visible from the street. Half the respondents saw it as advantage because they could see the layout of the premises before entering; the other half saw it as a disadvantage because they could be seen carrying out the robbery by other people on the outside.

A frequent comment was that robbers preferred targets that were located in areas with which they were familiar. Some robbers talked about returning to the area where they had grown up in order to select a target. As the research from The Netherlands had indicated, more professional robbers will normally be prepared to travel further afield in search of more lucrative targets, whereas more inexperienced robbers will tend to choose targets reasonably close to home (Koppen and Jansen 1998).

Probably the most important consideration in relation to location was the ease of escape. Even amongst those who carried out relatively spontaneous robberies some consideration of escape routes was evident. Amongst more professional robbers it was not unusual that more than one escape route would be mapped out prior to the robbery.

Vulnerability

The vulnerability of different premises was bound up in the eyes of the robbers with the level of security, the characteristics of the staff and the number and type of customers. The main security features robbers identified were security screens on the counter, the general layout and the number and type of doors. Reference was made in a number of interviews to the greater accessibility of open-plan designs, to the benefits of having only one door and to the disadvantages of revolving and double doors.

There are, of course, considerable variations in the layout of different commercial premises such as banks and building societies. The dilemma for such financial establishments is appearing to be customer friendly while making the premises as difficult to rob as possible. The internal layout of most commercial establishments is largely a reflection of this tension. However, some robbers appeared sensitive to those banks, building societies and the like that leaned away from security features and towards greater attractiveness for customers.

A greater ambivalence was expressed about the presence of security equipment, particularly in relation to alarms. Robbers generally expressed the view that whether alarms were audible or silent made very little difference since they felt they would have enough time to carry out the robbery and make an escape. In terms of video equipment it was widely felt that if suitable disguises were worn – hat, glasses, crash helmet and the like – or if the robber made a point of not looking directly into a camera, they would be safe. However, particularly in relation to the last strategy, there was often a lack of awareness of the distribution of cameras. As one interviewee explained: 'Well cameras is usually dud 'cos I'm masked up. But I did get caught on a hidden camera...I couldn't believe it. I was coming out and they've got me pulling the mask off...straight on me, very crafty.'

Of critical importance, particularly amongst the amateurs who relied on immediate visible impressions, was the type of staff working in the premises and their distribution, as well as the number of customers coming in and out of the premises. In relation to customers, the aim in most cases amongst the more inexperienced robbers was to wait until there were very few customers. Having waited for customer numbers to be at a minimum, some consideration was given to the type of customer – avoiding those who may cause a problem.

Modus operandi

Although the general format of a commercial robbery is relatively standard, there were found to be some interesting variations in exactly how different robberies were carried out. Different robbers have a distinctly different style that will involve a different form of demand, a different type of disguise and a different use of weapons. These differences tend to give those who engage in a number of robberies a particular 'trademark' that allows the police to link robberies together and, in some cases, to associate them with particular individuals.

In essence, there are five main variations of the modus operandi: 1) the presentation or the threat of a firearm at the screen; 2) jumping over the counter or getting behind the counter and threatening staff; 3) breaking into the premises when closed and opening the safe or waiting for staff to arrive; 4) threatening customers or taking a customer hostage; and 5) an inside job in which access is arranged beforehand.

There were a few other variations on these themes. For example, in one case a robber made an appointment with the manager in order to gain access to the 'secure' section of the premises behind the counter and then, while discussing a possible loan, he pulled out a gun and arranged a different type of withdrawal. The most frequent strategy was the presentation of a weapon or the threat of a weapon at the counter.

However, a number of the robbers interviewed preferred to take a hostage inside the premises, holding a gun against his or her head. They reported this gave them considerable leverage. Others, on the other hand, preferred, where possible, to leap over the counter to maximise control and to make sure the staff emptied all the tills. It was one of the differences between the amateurs and the more experienced robbers that the latter were able to maximise the takings and had learned that the cash may be in a number of places, including the safe. It was the ability to stay 'in control' for a longer period of time that allowed some of the more organised and persistent robbers to maximise the amount stolen. Recalling a bank robbery in Leicester, one respondent gave the following account:

My accomplice had the sawn-off shotgun, and I had the barrels tucked into my sleeve. It was the actual barrels of the gun. I gave the cashier the bag and told her to fill it. She bent down. I warned her not to activate any of the alarms and said; 'Just be a good girl, fill the bag and I won't hurt you'. She then filled it, entered the till and took the money off the counter. My co-accused had put his weapon down, dragging all the money off the counter and putting it into his pockets...I demanded money off another cashier and she said there wasn't any and I told her that there's some there: 'Don't fuck with me, I know it's there'. She bent down and gave me two parcels of money sealed up out of the reserve drawer....

Another ploy used in many financial establishments is slowly to fill the bag with notes of little value. This strategy is designed to slow down the process of handing over the cash and thereby reducing the amount of money taken by the more nervous robbers. Since the duration of the majority of robberies is only a few minutes, a delaying tactic can be effective. The more experienced robbers tend to demand 'twenties' and 'fifties'. In some cases the cashiers put in wads of largely blank paper into the bags to minimise loss. Similarly, in many financial establishments the alarm is triggered by removing a clip from the drawer. However, very few respondents had been caught by silent alarms being triggered in this way.

Attacks against cash-carrying operations can take one of five forms. They may involve attacks on the courier whilst carrying cash from the armoured vehicle to a particular premises. These are known in the trade as 'across the pavement' robberies. Secondly, the attack can take the form of the robber waiting inside the premises for a delivery of cash boxes. Thirdly, there is the direct attack on the security van in order to persuade the security staff to pass out the cash. Fourthly, there are what are often referred to as 'tiger kidnaps', in which the robbers take members of the guard's family hostage and threaten to hurt or kill them if the money is not handed over. Finally and more exceptionally, the security van itself is hijacked and driven away to be cut open later.

Reference was made during interviews to all these methods of attacking security vans. The most common form of attack was 'across the pavement' and there was only one 'tiger kidnap'. In this case a security van was intercepted in the Caledonian Road in north London and the robbers after overcoming the security guards, told them that they knew where they lived and that they were holding their families hostage. The address and the names of the family members were supplied and, consequently, the guards handed over the contents of the van, totalling approximately £1.5 million. It transpired that although the robbers had details of the guard's address and the names and ages of the members of his family they had not, in fact, kidnapped them. One interesting aspect of this case was that the £1.5 million was in newly minted notes with all the numbers running in sequence. The robbers attempted to launder the money through a market trader in Leicester who was caught when his son-in-law (who was given £50,000 to launder) walked straight into a building society and put the money on the counter and asked to open a deposit account. The cashier noticed the notes were sequential and rang the police. The man was arrested and so was his father-in-law.

There were a few other variations on these themes. Amongst the more memorable aspects of different modus operandi was one robber who always wore a very bright yellow top because he thought victims and witnesses would be drawn to it rather than looking at his face. He did not, however, consider that such a distinguishing jacket might make him more identifiable when leaving the premises. In other cases robbers stated they always fired a couple of rounds into the ceiling in order to persuade cashiers they meant business, while in other cases the 'trademark' was attacking the security screen with a hilti hammer and smashing it.

In selecting between targets and in carrying out the robbery, there are a number of more or less conscious considerations in play. However, different types of premises handle different amounts of money and have different levels of accessibility and vulnerability. In order to reduce vulnerability, many financial institutions have introduced a range of different crime prevention measures.

Preventing and reducing robberies

In 1986 a Working Group on Commercial Robbery carried out one of the first major reviews of commercial armed robberies in the UK (Home

Office 1986). The publication of the report was prompted by the reported growth of armed robberies in the mid-1980s in which the number of raids, the use of firearms and the amounts taken increased significantly – with the exception of post offices. Two major robberies had also been carried out by armed gangs in London in 1983. The first involved a Security Express raid in Shoreditch that netted over £6 million; while the second was the famous Brinks-Matt gold bullion robbery in which 6,800 bars of gold valued at £26 million were stolen from the Brinks-Matt security depot at Heathrow airport (Darbyshire and Hilliard 1993).

Because of the lack of information available the Working Group (Home Office 1986) carried out its own survey and found that raids against banks, building societies and cash-in-transit had doubled between 1983 and 1986 and that the amount stolen had increased by 50, 55 and 250 per cent, respectively. The police-generated data available at the time, although providing information about the number of robberies directed at particular targets, was of little use in identifying successful security measures. The Working Group's survey revealed that across the country there was a very uneven distribution of commercial robberies, with over half of all recorded bank robberies and approximately 60 per cent of building society robberies taking place in the London area, with other urban areas such as Manchester, Merseyside, the West Midlands and Bristol all experiencing a disproportionately high number of commercial robberies. Within this uneven geographical distribution there were found to be some significant variations between the types of commercial premises robbed, with one building society, for example, experiencing raids in 19 per cent of its branches compared to an average of 4.4 per cent for building societies as a whole.

The decrease in the number of raids directed towards post offices in this period was attributed to the introduction of various target-hardening devices, including the upgrading of security screens, the introduction of audible alarms and the general upgrading of physical security, particularly in high crime areas. Interestingly, in over 90 per cent of the cases in which audible alarms were set off the attacker fled.

The Working Group (ibid.) recommended more target hardening, although they were sensitive to considerations of cost and the need to make financial intuitions welcoming to customers. This is probably not surprising since the committee were mainly drawn from banks, insurance and various security companies. They advocated more cameras and the development of a more open-planned layout for financial institutions such as banks and building societies, as well as better training for staff together with a general decrease in the amounts of cash held in each branch.

To some extent the increases the Working Group had identified were a function of a growth in the number of outlets for financial institutions and in the number of security vehicles, as well as in the greater amount of money in circulation. However, the significant increase in the use of firearms associated with commercial robberies, as well as the growing attention that was being drawn to armed robberies as a result of a number of audacious and high-profile robberies, persuaded the authorities and financial institutions that something had to be done to tighten up security and to reduce vulnerability.

The array of measures currently available to financial institutions and retail outlets is considerable. The selection of different types of security measures will be governed by cost, suitability and assumptions about effectiveness. Table 3.2 shows the distribution of security measures that was in use by a sample of retail outlets in the mid-1990s.

Table 3.2: Use of security measures by different retail outlets.

Item	%
Intruder alarms	81.0
Five-lever locks	75.2
Toughened glass	64.3
Reinforced doors	52.6
Bars/grilles on windows	53.5
Fake note detector	54.3
Security lights	42.4
Safe	37.5
Staff training on security	34.0
Bars/grilles on doors	46.7
Shutters	41.0
Fencing	28.1
Gatekeeper/receptionist working hours	12.8
Barbed wire	19.1
Intercom entry	14.8
Internal CCTV	24.3
Post-coding equipment	16.2
Roof protection	15.1
Gatekeeper/receptionist outside hours	6.0
Anti-climb paint	5.7
External CCTV	4.9
Dog on premises	2.6
Tagging of stock	2.9
Store detectives	2.0

Source: Wood et al (1996).

A subsequent Home Office publication that looked specifically at building societies found two features that significantly affected the difference between successful and unsuccessful robberies: the nature of the branch's security screens and the presence of members of the public (Austin 1988). The main reason why the absence of customers was important was not so much that it put potential robbers off but that members of staff were instructed that, when there was no danger to members of the public they should simply walk away from the counter. Some consideration was also given to reducing the offender's sense of control rather than concentrating on target-hardening measures. It was suggested that introducing greater unpredictability into the robbery by reducing the offender's ability to communicate or to keep track on the movements of all the staff may increase the offender's sense of uncertainty at the scene of the crime. As Walsh (1986a) pointed out, anything that can be done to increase the number and variety of imponderables complicates matters for the robbers and may reduce the chances of the attack being successful. A version of this type of strategy was adopted by the National Westminster Bank group in the early 1990s. During the previous decade this bank had adopted a policy of not disputing the demands of robbers and had instructed its staff always to comply and hand over the money. Consequently, the bank gained a reputation as an easy target and as a bank that always likes to say 'yes'. However, it adopted a radically different policy in the early 1990s and instructed its staff to fall to the floor out of sight when faced with an armed robber. As a result the robber stood bewildered and impotent and, as the footage from the video cameras located in these banks revealed, the frustrated robber normally walked or ran straight out of the premises. Admittedly, this particular strategy was only possible because the counters had been fitted with tall bullet-proof screens that protected the staff and served to prevent the robber from jumping over the counter, but as a crime prevention measure it was much more effective than adopting the target-hardening measures which some banks were applying at the time. As a result of this initiative the National Westminster Bank ceased to be the league leader amongst the banks targeted for robbery and, subsequently, became one of the least victimised high-street banks.

However, this promising strategy for reducing the likelihood of successful robberies (which was based on an understanding of the motivation of armed robbers) was generally sidelined in favour of the more fashionable situational crime prevention measures. Despite the fact that the available evidence, even in the mid-1980s, had indicated the limits of alarms, cameras and different types of interior design, these situational measures predominated. Using rational choice theory as its 'theoretical' justification, more money was poured into target-hardening

55

and security packages. The drive continually to increase security measures was limited either by escalating costs or the fear of turning these financial and commercial establishments into unwelcoming fortresses. Rational choice theory, as has been suggested in Chapter 2, had little to say that was very useful about offender motivation and was, in effect, better seen as a form of 'rational defence theory' concerned with reducing the vulnerability and accessibility of targets. However, even in this respect it provided a limited response because it drew on the commonsense wisdom that if you make targets harder to access and reduce the potential rewards to offenders, you will reduce the propensity to rob. The lack of any sophisticated theoretical dimensions to this approach did not, however, make it any less appealing to security personnel and policy-makers. In fact, its avoidance of theoretical complexities and its blatant pragmatism formed a major part of its appeal.

Before going on to examine the deployment of situational measures during the 1990s, it may be appropriate at this point to indulge in a brief digression in order to consider the possible differences between forms of crime prevention that do involve some understanding of motivation, on the one hand, and those that are based on rational choice theory or routine activities theory and the like that take motivation as a given. In many ways the experience of dealing with graffiti on the New York subway is instructive when considering the relative significance of motivational questions in relation to the formulation of crime-reduction strategies.

During the 1980s the New York subway became a target for graffiti artists and, as a consequence, of a number of target-hardening measures were introduced mainly in the form of anti-graffiti paint. But the graffiti artists (being reasonably creative) found ways to overcome this obstacle and to use paint that would stick to these new surfaces. As more anti-graffiti measures were introduced the graffiti artists found a way around them (Sloan-Hewitt and Kelling 1992).[1] However, those who began to examine the motivations of graffiti artists realised that the whole point of graffiti is 'getting up'. That is, the over-riding aim is to make sure the graffiti is seen. Responding to this insight, a strategy was instigated in New York whereby all graffiti was removed from the subway trains and the trains were not allowed to leave the depot until cleaned. By destroying the logic of graffiti this strategy succeeded where the situational strategy failed. It was a consequence of thinking smarter rather than engaging in escalating and ultimately self-defeating target-hardening strategy.

Such insights were lost on the policy-makers and the security personnel who took the responsibility for combating armed robbery in the 1980s and early 1990s. Consequently much time, effort and expense was expended during this period in the UK developing new target-hardening measures. Amongst the most notable were rising screens and better quality surveillance and video equipment, as well as double entrance doors and automatic alarm systems. The increased use of the automated cash-removal systems and the spread of credit card facilities meant that many financial and commercial institutions felt better protected and more secure.

The measures introduced to protect cash-in-transit were probably amongst the most elaborate. Dummy boxes and bags were increasingly incorporated into the deliveries such that even if a robber grabbed two or three bags in a raid the chances were that one or two would contain only shredded paper. Alternatively, some cash boxes contained dye so that if they were opened incorrectly the dye would spill over the money, rendering it unusable. Other boxes (if not opened properly) emitted coloured smoke. Probably the most imaginative crime prevention strategy involved a number of metal non-retractable prongs protruding from the money box if an attempt was made to force it open. The aim of this device was to pin the robber in the seat of the getaway car until he or she could be apprehended.

The displacement of robbery

Even in cases where situational crime prevention measures are credited with reducing the number of robberies, or the amount stolen, there is always the question of whether displacement takes place. Displacement can take a number of forms, including a change of location (geographical); a change in time (temporal); a change in the modus operandi (tactical); a change in target; or it may involve the selection of a completely different type of crime (Reppetto 1976). The Working Group on Commercial Robbery (Home Office 1986) made some reference to how the perceived changes in the security systems that had been introduced into banks, building societies and post offices appeared to lead to an increase in raids against cash carriers. Clare Austin (1988) noted the tendency for robbers to select those premises that have fewer protective measures or a small number of visible staff. Alternatively, the implementation of general security measures may result in 'escalation', encouraging robbers to use more force or to take hostages.

In the literature on displacement there are two central concerns: the first is whether the implementation of crime prevention measures will result in the escalation towards more serious and violent robberies or, alternatively, lead to the deflection of robberies towards more vulnerable targets. The second, related, concern refers to the issue of whether crime prevention interventions result in malign or benign forms of displacement. Robert Barr and Ken Pease (1990) have argued that displacement may take positive or negative forms without actually reducing the overall level of crime. Alternatively, there is the suggestion that in contrast to the negative or malign effects of displacement there is a possibility of a 'diffusion of benefits' resulting from intervention. That is, crime prevention efforts may produce unexpected beneficial effects by reducing crime in adjacent areas or for related targets (Clarke and Weisburd 1994).

In relation to the issue of escalation there are a number of international studies that have attempted to throw some light on this question. Christian Grandjean's (1990) Swiss study on bank robberies found that banks who had protected their tellers with bullet-proof screens reduced the risk of robbery and the risk of violence to staff. There was, he claims, little evidence of displacement from banks to other targets such as post offices, but there was some evidence that increased security had effected a displacement from more to less protected banks. This study by Grandjean reflects some of the difficulties of trying to assess the displacement effect of target-hardening interventions. His finding that there was no 'escalation' effect is hardly surprising since only a limited number of banks had bullet-proof security screens and it would seem likely that given the wide selection of targets available, the majority of robbers would select banks that appeared more vulnerable. The observation that there seemed to be some displacement from more to less well protected targets endorses this possibility. The claim, however, that there was little evidence of displacement to other targets such as post offices is stretching credibility since he admits that post offices do not really provide an alternative target for bank robbers because the expected takings are so low. The alternative target for bank robbers, he notes, is likely to be cash-in-transit and the figures he supplies in fact show that when the number of bank robberies went down robberies against security vehicles went up and, in a later period when attacks on security vehicles decreased, bank robberies started to increase again. Thus based on his own figures the target-hardening strategies he identifies appear to have displacement effects of the type that might reasonably be predicted. The fact that bank robberies as a whole continued to increase following the introduction of these target-hardening measures suggests that, while there may have been benefits for individual banks, for the industry as a whole there was little gain.

Although the actual findings are less positive that Grandjean would like to believe, there are two methodological limitations in this research that should be noted. The first is that the overall sample was relatively small (152) and the second that fluctuations in the distribution of armed robberies can be influenced by many other factors besides displacement, such as the number of active robbers working in an area over time. Whether one considers the interventions in Switzerland as 'benign' or 'malign' depends largely on the position from which you assess displacement. For the banks that had screens installed there were probably benefits in terms of a reduced number of robberies and an increased sense of security by staff, at least in the short term. For the other banks and the security firms that were the 'beneficiaries' of this process of displacement, the interventions were almost certainly seen in negative terms. From an independent vantage point, however, the wider distribution of robberies might be seen as benign inasmuch as it 'at least shares the agony around' (Barr and Pease 1990).

An informative discussion of the potential 'escalation' effects of introducing target-hardening measures in commercial premises is provided by Paul Ekblom (1987) in his examination of the target-hardening strategies introduced into the UK in the 1980s to reduce attacks against sub-post offices. Ekblom provides a more sophisticated analysis of escalation and displacement than most other studies and he notes the important methodological point that target-hardening measures are often introduced when the problem is at its peak and therefore would be likely to decrease in many cases irrespective of the effectiveness of any particular measure. He also points out that many planned robberies are not in fact carried out once the robbers enter the premises and that they may be put off by a variety of considerations. Thus, the number of attempted or unsuccessful robberies is likely to be underestimated, although the number of aborted robberies can have a significant impact upon the success, or otherwise, of particular interventions.

Given these methodological caveats, Ekblom (ibid.) claims the new security screens that were introduced into sub-post offices in the early 1980s were responsible for the recorded reduction in the number of raids. However, he notes that robbers have adopted other methods of attack, principally in the form of firearms threats at the screen. He maintains that the greater reliance on firearms does not constitute a mode of escalation because robbers' 'naive faith in the weapon may prevent them from adequately preparing for the raid', thus increasing the likelihood of failure. The overall reduction in the number of robberies has not worsened the 'plight of the staff in exposing them to more failed attacks'; similarly, by encouraging offenders to carry guns, staff are less likely to 'have a go'. However, research on the use of firearms in robberies suggests these robberies are significantly more likely to result in fatalities (Cook 1982). Thus although the improved screens may have decreased the overall number of successful robberies, they have almost certainly increased the risk of fatalities amongst post office staff. These measures have, Ekblom (1987) admits, also probably displaced attacks to other similar commercial targets such as building societies. Thus the intervention may have had some benefit in post offices in general, but the increased reliance on the deployment of firearms by robbers is unlikely to be perceived as a form of benign displacement by post office staff.

This is not to suggest an inevitability about escalation or the displacement effects of interventions. Clearly, the reduced amounts of cash most commercial organisations now carry have almost certainly reduced the takings from robberies, if not actually reducing the number of robberies (Clarke and McGrath 1990). But even these strategies may have their downside in that they may put more pressure on staff who are unable to open time-locked safes, or who are able only to hand over paltry sums of money when threatened with firearms and are consequently put under pressure to find more money quickly.

A central point of reference for international discussions on the effectiveness of target-hardening strategies in commercial premises has been in relation to measures introduced in Australia and Canada in the late 1980s (Challinger 1989). Australian-based research found that some 5 per cent of its 6,000 banks were robbed in 1988 and that there was an uneven distribution of bank robberies across the country and between different banking organisations (Marsden 1990). As part of a defensive strategy against armed robbery, target-hardening measures were introduced, and the citing and interior layout of banks were reviewed. Based on the work of Ron Clarke and his colleagues (1990), an attempt was made to model risk factors, and security screens were introduced in one in three banks. The effect was a reduction in the number of robberies against the banks that had screens installed but the robberies that did take place were found to be more likely to be carried out by a gang rather than an individual and were more likely to involve loaded firearms, while the amounts taken were generally higher. In short, this strategy resulted in an escalation and generally put the staff at greater risk because the armed robbers aimed to get behind the counter. It may well also have encouraged those robbers who had fixed monetary goals to carry out a greater number of robberies (Gabor et al 1987). There was also found to be some displacement from the better protected branches to the less well protected branches. In a somewhat understated conclusion the author of the report on this intervention concluded that 'security screens are not the last word in protection' (Marsden 1990). The same study also concluded that cameras were not shown to have a deterrent effect and that the presence of security guards in branches had a fairly immediate and local displacement effect. Consequently the report calls for an industry-wide strategy rather than each banking group developing its own initiatives, since this is likely to have adverse consequences on other banks. In reviewing the effectiveness of target-hardening measures in

Australia since the 1980s, Marsden (ibid.: 10) concludes: 'In summary, target hardening of the Australian banks from the early 1980s onwards does not appear to have shifted bank robberies onto other targets, although there is good evidence of displacement between more or less protected branches and between banking groups.'

The Canadian experience during the 1980s took a different form. One study located in Montreal during 1981–82 involved sample of 1,019 bank robberies and it was found there was little association between the security ratings of banks and the numbers of times they were victimised. This may be, the authors note, because the level of security was itself a result of the bank's proneness to armed robbery (Gabor *et al* 1987). In a second study carried out by the same researchers on convenience stores, it was found that the level of robbery was virtually the same amongst the group with the highest level of security as that amongst those with a minimum degree of security. The conclusion of the study was that 'security measures may have only a negligible effect upon the choice of target' and that 'robbers, on the whole, are not as responsive to security measures, and hence in choosing a target as advocates of opportunity reduction approaches might think' (Gabor 1989).[2] Similar conclusions were reached by James Calder and John Bauer (1992) in their study of convenience store robberies in San Antonio, Texas.

There is a considerable amount of US literature that discusses the effectiveness of different forms of intervention employed to reduce robberies on convenience stores. Convenience stores that open late and that normally have only one member of staff working at any one time provide accessible and relatively unprotected targets (Duffala 1976). Consequently convenience stores such as 7-Eleven are unsurprisingly amongst the most victimised commercial targets in America. The average take from these robberies is $300–$400 and the main cost arises from injury compensation claims and loss of qualified employees (Hunter 1991).

Much of the debate over the last decade concerning convenience stores has been over whether there should be a requirement by law that there should be at least two people working at any one time in order to increase protection while making a robbery more difficult to carry out. Views on the introduction of two staff have been split, with companies claiming this would create higher costs and may not deter prospective robbers, while advocates of 'double staffing' argue it would afford greater protection to staff. The latter quote the studies that have been conducted that show that an overwhelming percentage of robberies have been carried out in stores with only one member of staff on duty (Bellamy 1995). Only Florida, however, has introduced legislation in the form of the Convenience Store Security Act 1990 to enforce double staffing in convenience stores, while other states have relied upon a range of crime

61

prevention measures such as improving lighting, increasing the number of cameras, making less cash available, putting in more alarms, restricting parking and increasing the vigilance of staff. The use of these different security strategies does appear to have had some effect on the number and distribution of convenience store robberies as well as on the amount of money taken. It was, however, clear from the debate over the deployment of security in convenience stores that the owners, by and large, preferred to spend their money on physical security rather than on employing additional members of staff.

Conclusion

Armed robbery is a precarious business, particularly when there is little planning. Robbers have adopted a number of strategies to commit this apparently straightforward crime. In pursuing their often loosely formulated objectives, commercial robbers have adapted to the changing forms of security that have been introduced at considerable cost over the last 30 years. The introduction of cameras and alarms has encouraged the more experienced robbers to use disguises, to limit their time on the premises or to change their modus operandi. The more desperate and disorganised robbers, however, seem largely impervious to these 'sophisticated' security measures and they continue to attack targets they believe to be vulnerable. This is not to say that some crime prevention measures have not had some effect. Given the enormous amount of money and effort spent in developing and implementing these measures, it would be churlish to suggest they have been ineffective. However, these effects are often localised and short term and, in most cases, they are considerably less than is assumed, while in some instances they are clearly counterproductive. The more effective crime prevention measures tend to be those that involve thinking smarter, rather than entering into the expensive spiral of target hardening, in which the recognised limitations of the existing measures do not become an argument for rethinking, but rather serve as a justification for extending target hardening. Those interventions that can address issues of motivation and that aim to destroy the logic of the robbery are more likely to be effective. Thus, for example, the deceptively simple strategy of dropping to the floor when confronted by a robber appears to have been very successful in certain banks and building societies in reducing robberies, and it prevents robbers from taking 'control'. Similarly, interior layouts that maximise uncertainty and that promote variation are likely to be of more use in deterring prospective robbers than bullet-proof screens or alarms.

The displacement effects of the various target-hardening and crime prevention measures are difficult to assess, particularly since fluctuations in the rate and distribution of armed robbery can be caused by a wide range of factors, apart from crime prevention measures. From a review of the changes that have taken place in armed robbery in England and Wales between 1982–1995 and it would appear that the overall rate has decreased from a peak in 1982 and that there has been a redistribution between and within different types of targets – generally from the better protected to the least protected. These developments are neither clearly malign or benign and there is little evidence of a 'diffusion of benefits'. There is, however, some evidence that the numbers of commercial robberies have decreased in relation to both Band 1 and Band 2 targets in recent years in the UK. There are many who would like to claim these decreases are a function of target-hardening measures, particularly those who have authorised or benefited from the considerable expenditure that has been spent on these interventions. However, since armed robberies have decreased in relation to targets that have minimal levels of physical security, the reasons for the decrease appear to be more to do with the changing motivations of offenders and the changing trajectories of their criminal careers.

Notes

1 It is a little ironic that Ron Clarke includes Sloan-Hewitt and George Kelling's account of the failure of situational measures to reduce graffiti on the New York subway system in his book on *Situational Crime Prevention: Successful Case Studies* (1997) since it involves an implicit critique of Clarke's own position.

2 In this study, Thomas Gabor (1989) examined a seven-step crime prevention strategy developed by the Southland Corporation who own the 7-Eleven chain of convenience stores. These steps involve, in essence, the increased use of surveillance, target hardening and reducing the available cash on the premises. In the 60 American stores in which this programme was tried, it was claimed there had been a 30 per cent reduction in robberies in the first six months. However, when this strategy was introduced to its Canadian stores, the 7-Eleven stores experienced a 20–25 per cent increase in robberies during the first year the measures were introduced. These results suggest that the context in which measures are introduced can have profound effect on their effectiveness (see Pawson and Tilley 1997).

Chapter 4

Weapon use in robbery

Introduction

When we think about robbery we tend to think about firearms. There are good reasons for making this connection. In 1995 robberies accounted for three quarters of all recorded offences involving firearms (other than air guns) in England and Wales (Home Office 2000). In America, the association between firearms and robberies is even more pronounced with approximately 660,000 robberies reported in 1993, of which 42 per cent involved firearms (Wintemunte 2000). In New York City alone 91,000 robberies were reported in 1992, and guns were used in 40 per cent of these incidents (Zimring and Hawkins 1997). However, when examining the relation between firearms and commercial robberies, it is important to bear in mind that other weapons besides firearms are regularly used and that firearms themselves come in a number of different forms. To lose sight of the diversity of the weapons employed to carry out this offence is to blur the meaning of the central concept of 'armed' in relation to robberies and, consequently, to treat all 'armed robberies' as homogeneous events, thus overlooking important differences in offender motivation as well as the differential impact of different weapons on victims.

To unpack the significance of 'armed' robbery, this chapter addresses a number of key issues associated with the weapons used by commercial robbers including the reasons why they choose different types of weapon, the trends in weapon choice over time, the relation between weapon choice and the selection of targets, the use of firearms by the police, the impact of gun control measures on the availability of illegal firearms and, finally, the effects of weapon choice on the sentencing of those convicted of armed robbery.

Weapon choice and acquisition

Philip Cook (1976) – who employs a 'strategic choice analysis' based on the conception of the robber as a rational economic calculator – argues that robbers carry guns because it allows them to rob more lucrative targets and to maximise their takings. The research evidence from the UK suggests that weapon choice is less 'rational' than Cook believes, and that it is conditioned by a number of factors, including pragmatism, habit, utility and even fashion.

There can be little doubt there is some association between the choice of weapon and the amount of money sought. However, this association is generally weak and uncertain. For the majority of robbers in our prison sample, it was not only the pursuit of certain targets or the amount of money sought that determined the choice of weapon. As noted above, the selection of targets is often contingent and, in the majority of cases, robbers have little idea of what their actual take might be. A number of robbers who were interviewed said they were motivated by the acquisition of a firearm. In one case the 'escalation' from commercial burglaries to bank robberies occurred as a result of finding two shotguns by chance. As the robber explained: 'We was doing well with the money 'cos we was doing quite a few commercial burglaries...and then we came across the shotguns and that made us like six feet two – made us feel big. We decided to get some big money – more bravado than anything else.' Thus rather than seeing the robber as a rational economic actor dedicated to the maximisation of rewards, we found in this and other cases that weapon choice was subject to the vagaries of availability. Other robbers indicated their weapon choice was influenced by their previous exposure to and familiarity with different kinds of weapons and by their concerns with the injuries that might be sustained by themselves or their victims.

Clearly acquiring such weapons as clubs, knives, axes and the like is relatively straightforward, and research shows that many young people in the UK carry knives and other weapons routinely (Quinn 1996). It was also evident in our sample of convicted robbers that around 20 per cent had spent some time in the army during which they had learnt how to use firearms and had developed a familiarity with different kinds of weapons. Time spent in the army had also fostered proclivities towards violence and the engagement in high-risk activities, albeit within an institutionalised and disciplined framework. The acquisition of firearms poses a somewhat more difficult problem, depending on the type of firearm sought. In general, our interviewees who had real firearms stated they had acquired them through a friend or an accomplice. A few had bought them on the black market or through gun dealers. Two of the more professional robbers admitted acquiring guns through organised burglaries.

In some cases these guns were purchased; in others they were rented for a short period. Normally, obvious markings had been removed and the guns were disposed of soon after the robbery. There was a division amongst respondents between those who acquired a firearm temporarily and those who kept the same firearm over a long period. Although the latter group were clearly in the minority, there were those career robbers who possessed cherished firearms and who kept them specifically for use in armed robbery. In one such case a robber was caught on a conspiracy charge after a neighbour spotted him regularly cleaning his guns in his garage on Sunday mornings. A significant number of interviewees said they had used deactivated weapons or old guns that were not capable of firing a lethal shot and that were relics from the war. Others admitted using replicas or imitation firearms.

There was a distinction between offenders who might be described as 'weapon specialists' and those who were 'weapon eclectic'. The available evidence suggests that the majority of robbers are weapon eclectic and that those who carried replica guns on their last robbery will have tended to have used real guns or indeed other types of weapon in the past (Wright and Rossi 1985; Morrison and O'Donnell 1994). This apparent lack of weapon specialism seems to arise either because robbers who have used real guns in the past realise an imitation gun is adequate for the task or because they now have more confidence and no longer feel they require the support of a real gun to go through with the robbery. Alternatively, it may have been the case that real guns were not readily available when required.

In one study carried out by the Home Office in 1998 that attempted to discover what level of access offenders have to firearms, it was found that, amongst a sample of arrestees in Sunderland and Nottingham, 8 per cent of those interviewed in Nottingham said they had owned a gun recently, while a further 9 per cent said they had access to a gun in the recent past. In Sunderland only 3 per cent admitted to owning a gun recently and 14 per cent to having access to a gun (Bennett 2000). This study indicates a relatively low level of gun ownership in both locations and that access to guns, even among known offenders, is limited (Bryan 2000).

Although most of our respondents claimed they could get hold of a real firearm if they wanted to, the reality appears to be, in Britain at least, that real firearms are considerably more difficult to acquire than is often imagined, and that robbers resort to replica guns or other kinds of weapons because they can purchase them easily and because they are relatively inexpensive. Given that many robberies are fairly spontaneous events with limited planning, robbers who do not keep their own supply of firearms may find it very difficult to get hold of the gun they want at a price they can afford. Blank-firing replicas, on the other hand, are widely advertised in British gun magazines and can be purchased over the counter for as little as £20 through the numerous gun dealerships across the country (Taylor and Hornsby 2000). This cost compares to around £250 for a handgun, £600–£750 for a sawn-off shotgun and about £1,500 for an automatic, such as an Uzi.

Apart from issues of access and price there are a number of considerations that may influence weapon choice. Some robbers we spoke to had a preference for clubs and axes which, they felt, were useful in smashing down screens and partitions while frightening victims and bystanders into compliance. The sheer volume of noise that could be produced by these weapons was seen to provide a demonstration of the strength and determination of the robber. Knives, which are also regularly used in commercial robberies in the UK, provide an easily concealable weapon that makes little noise but can instil considerable fear.

Firearms, however, have a number of definite advantages over other weapons. Principally, firearms allow control at a distance. This makes it easier to control a number of different people simultaneously. Unlike the knife or the club, the gun allows a considerable degree of impersonality, involving little or no physical contact between the offender and the victim. The gun, as they say, is also a great leveller. It makes the weak strong. Even in the hands of the unskilled assailant the presentation of a firearm can be used to show he means business.

How convincing robbers are during the robbery will, in part, be a function of the type of weapon they are carrying and their demeanour. Clearly a robber wielding sawn-off shotguns presents a daunting image while those with smaller handguns may appear less frightening. In cases where the weapons involved appear to be replicas, or where they are simply 'implied', the level of fear and the trauma of the victim are likely to be less. Most victims and witnesses will tend to be aware that the size, type and calibre of the firearm make a considerable difference in the amount of physical damage that might be incurred and, correspondingly, the degree of lethality (Cook 1991).

The decision over which type of weapon to choose may also be linked to considerations of self-defence. A number of robbers indicated they carried particular weapons either to protect themselves from 'have-a-go' heroes or from the police. Thus, for example, while some robbers did not feel it necessary to carry a loaded firearm to carry out the robbery, firearms had considerable utility in facilitating escape when it 'came on top', or when confronted by the police. One robber, who admitted carrying a loaded sawn-off shotgun on his last robbery, was asked under what conditions he would be prepared to use it. He replied:

I suppose mainly under siege conditions; but even then I don't think I would have deliberately set out to hurt someone...mainly just use it as a deterrent or as a means to escape...firing into the floor or into the air as a warning...[However] I wouldn't hesitate to hurt the police. I wouldn't hesitate at all, because I know it would either be them or me, and I would sooner it was one of them.

A number of robbers interviewed felt the police were just waiting for an opportunity to shoot them and cited various cases in which people they knew or whom they had heard of had been shot by the police while carrying out a robbery or while trying to escape. Accounts of such shootings were no doubt part of the folk wisdom amongst prisoners, but it was clear they believed the police were regularly armed and that they would not hesitate to shoot given the opportunity.

Another factor that has been shown to influence weapon choice is the nature of offender motivation and, particularly, their predisposition towards violence. In James Wright and Peter Rossi's (1985) study on armed criminals in the USA (which was based upon interviews with incarcerated felons) the authors found that carrying real firearms put offenders in control and provided a degree of flexibility. An important advantage of carrying a real firearm, it was felt, was that victim resistance would be minimal and no one would get hurt. At the same time it was claimed amongst those who did not carry a real firearm that this decision was based on the desire to minimise the risk of injuries either to victims or to themselves. Amongst this group, carrying a real firearm was seen to be 'just asking for trouble', or that carrying a real gun 'just didn't seem right', and would result in receiving a longer sentence, if caught. In some cases they simply stated they had never owned a gun and would not know how to use one.

Interestingly, there is an overlap in rationales between the gun carriers and the non-gun carriers in that both groups made their choices largely on the basis of avoiding rather than perpetuating violence, while protecting themselves. Thus Wright and Rossi (ibid.) conclude that the decision to carry a real gun may have less to do with the general availability of firearms, knowledge of firearms and the price of the gun and more to do with reducing risks and the possible sanctions.

Trends in weapon use

Changes in the choice of weapons over time provides important clues to changes in the nature of armed robbery itself, to the forms of motivation and to the modus operandi of offenders. It has been found that the mean annual number of recorded armed robberies in England and Wales in which a firearm was involved was 35 in 1950. By the 1960s it had increased to 170, to 560 by the 1970s and to 1,340 by the 1980s. This rapid increase in the use of firearms reflected the shift from craft crime to project crime and the general target hardening of commercial premises that made the presentation of a firearm at the screen the typical form of commercial robbery (Greenwood 1983, 1986). The number of robberies that involved knives increased from over 1,000 in 1970s to about 3,000 by the 1980s, while the number of clubs and hammers used remained relatively stable over this period, at around 500 per annum (Home Office 1973; Harding 1979).

A number of trends associated with weapon use in commercial robberies are discernible over the past two decades. These involve the four related processes of decentralisation, deskilling, democratisation and downsizing. For example, over the past few years there has been a decrease in the proportion of commercial robberies in the UK involving firearms. In the early 1980s London accounted for almost 70 per cent of robberies involving firearms. By 1992 it had dropped to under 50 per cent. This change was not a result of a decrease or levelling off in robberies in the capital during the 1980s but the faster rate of increase in commercial robberies in other areas. Between 1982 and 1992, the number of recorded commercial robberies in London increased by 36 per cent; in other areas in England and Wales it increased by over 70 per cent.

Probably the most pronounced overall effect of the increased use of firearms in conjunction with commercial robberies has been a gradual process of deskilling. Craft crime required a certain degree of skill and organisation. The increased use of firearms, replicas and in some cases implied weapons means that armed robbery can be carried out with minimum level of preparation or organisation.

The third and related trend involves democratisation. Because little skill, training or organisation are needed to engage in commercial robbery and because a firearm is seen as sufficient in most cases to carry through a robbery, armed robbery has become a form of crime virtually anybody who is brave enough or desperate enough to take the chance on can commit. The increased use of implied firearms and imitation guns means that those contemplating a robbery do not even need to take the trouble to find or to learn how to use a gun.

Another identifiable trend in recent years involves the downsizing of the firearms used in armed robbery. This involves a reduction in the use of shotguns and the increased use of handguns, both real and imitation. Indicatively, the number of handguns involved in robberies in England and Wales more than doubled between 1986 and 1996, while the use of shotguns (which had become an increasingly popular weapon amongst armed robbers during the 1980s) halved over the same period. This shift in the choice of weapon appears to reflect a decrease in the number of old-style professional robbers and an increasing proportion of younger and less experienced offenders. Shotguns are unwieldy and expensive, whether long barrelled or sawn-off. They convey a message of harm maximisation rather than harm avoidance. Shotguns express a different type of commitment to violence from handguns. Their use also suggests differences of motivation. They are not the weapon of the young, spontaneous or aspiring robber who wants an easily concealable, smart, cheap weapon that is easy to handle. Smaller and smarter handguns are increasingly being marketed for their appearance and are seen in some circles as something of a fashion accessory (Blumstein 1994; Diaz 1999). This represents a further indication of deskilling and a movement away from the use of weapons that require care and commitment to those that are readily accessible and disposable. It is indicative that between the proportion of weapons used in robberies described as 'imitation', 'supposed' or 'other' firearms in the criminal statistics, these constitute a much higher proportion of the firearms associated with robbery between 1986 and 1996. It is also significant that firearms were reported to have been used in 11.7 per cent of robberies in 1991 and that this had decreased to 4.4 per cent by 1998. Thus the number of offences in the UK involving firearms has been steadily decreasing, and the proportion of firearms-related commercial robberies has also gone down (see Table 4.1).

In much of the foregoing discussion we have drawn upon official criminal statistics on firearms, but since over half the firearms used in robberies are not recovered and in some cases not seen clearly, the official statistics have to be treated with some caution. Apart from the few occasions in which firearms are discharged during a robbery or recovered afterwards by the police, there is no way of knowing exactly what type of weapon was used and classification is based largely on the descriptions provided by victims and witnesses. One implication of the reliance on the descriptions of witnesses and on the weapons recovered is a tendency to underestimate the proportion of imitation and 'supposed' firearms.

A detailed investigation of the firearms used in armed robbery was carried out in the early 1990s by Shona Morrison and Ian O'Donnell (1994). The authors interviewed 88 convicted armed robbers and found that 17 per cent had used a real handgun loaded with live ammunition, and that 24 per cent admitted to using a sawn-off shotgun (of which two thirds were loaded and six were unloaded). In 37 per cent of cases, the robber produced nothing, simply implying he possessed a gun. Indeed, amongst the weapons used to simulate a firearm were a courgette, a tube

Table 4.1: Number of robberies recorded by the police in England and Wales in which firearms were reported to have been used (by type of principal weapon).

Year	All weapons	All weapons excluding air weapon	Long-barrelled shotgun	Sawn-off shotgun	Hand gun	Rifle	Imitation firearm	Supposed firearm	Other firearm	Air weapon
1988	2,688	2,586	241	451	1,321	12	185	334	42	102
1989	3,390	3,300	280	524	1,772	10	235	438	41	90
1990	3,939	3,817	280	448	2,233	27	279	511	39	122
1991	5,296	5,140	381	650	2,988	28	314	735	44	156
1992	5,859	5,708	407	605	3,568	20	276	779	53	151
1993	6,012	5,881	440	603	3,670	20	236	875	37	131
1994	4,239	4,124	278	386	2,479	16	203	680	82	115
1995	4,206	4,094	245	299	2,647	14	169	644	76	112
1996	4,013	3,932	237	247	2,575	11	178	538	146	81
1997	3,029	2,930	121	178	1,854	10	186	460	121	99
1997–98	2,939	2,836	98	168	1,811	9	190	447	113	103
1998–99	2,973	2,890	138	193	1,814	4	163	419	159	83

Source: Criminal Statistics 1998 (Home Office 2000).

of toothpaste and a candle. In sum, the proportion of the interviewees who carried a weapon that was capable of firing a lethal shot was 35 per cent; only 17 per cent of all the robbers they interviewed, on the other hand, carried a genuine loaded firearm.

This finding puts a very different complexion on the meaning of 'armed' robbery and confirms the findings presented a few years earlier by Adrian Maybanks (1992) who analysed the weapons recovered by the Metropolitan Police following armed robberies. Maybanks found that out of 657 firearms, 375 were real while 282 were found to be imitation. Of the 657, only 5 had been discharged and these were more likely to be discharged in security van robberies (Maybanks and Yardley 1992).

In our own research (which also drew upon Metropolitan Police data) it was evident there was no consistent relation between the type of target and the weapons used. As Table 4.2 shows, even in cases involving security van robberies, a significant number of robberies were carried out without a firearm being shown. It is also interesting to note that in 10 per cent of betting shop robberies and 12 per cent of building society robberies, a firearm was not in evidence at all. In most cases knives were used but they also involved other weapons such as hammers and baseball bats. Out of a total of some 240 cases, handguns were used in approximately 50 per cent of robberies.

There is no clear relation between weapon choice and type of target in this sample of cases, nor was there a consistent relationship between the weapon used and amount of money sought or taken, although the sample is highly selective in that it includes only Band 1 robberies and, therefore, relatively well protected but potentially lucrative targets. In 17 of the cases more than one weapon was used and in these cases the amount taken has been divided accordingly.

Out of the 240 cases in our sample, 35 involved shotguns (either sawn-off or long barrelled) and the average take from shotgun robberies was £6,400. Of the 126 cases involving what were known or believed to be real handguns, the average amount stolen was £52,924. This average was massively inflated by a small number of robberies involving millions of pounds each. If these exceptional robberies are removed from the calculation the average handgun robbery is £9,360. The average take from robberies in which the weapon was merely implied was £9,640. The take again from robberies involving implied firearms was inflated by one exceptionally large haul and, if this robbery is excluded from the calculation the average drops to £4,260. There was one security van robbery that netted £2.3 million in which firearms were not used at all. In this case the robbers used a 14 lb hammer and an angle grinder. If this

Table 4.2: *Number and type of guns used against different targets in the Metropolitan Police Department.*

Target	No. of cases	Shotgun (known or believed real)	Handgun (known or believed real)	Known imitation	Implied firearm	Other (knife, club, etc.)
Security van	30	4	17	0	8	1
Bank	54	11	27	2	13	1
Building society	42	3	18	3	13	5
Post office	28	5	16	2	5	0
Betting shop	71	8	38	4	15	7
Jewellers	11	3	7	1	0	0

robbery is removed from the calculation the robberies that did not involve firearms at all netted a respectable £3,330.

In his study of armed robbery in Leicestershire and Northamptonshire, Michael Creedon (1992) found that handguns accounted for approximately 40 per cent of the weapons used. The second most prevalent weapons used were knives, which were used in about 25 per cent of commercial robberies. Clubs were identified in 15 per cent of cases, shotguns were used in less than 5 per cent of cases, while imitation firearms were used in approximately 5 per cent of cases. Creedon's findings indicate there is considerable regional variation in weapon use and that where the analysis involves data on all known robberies in the area, the profile of weapons is more mixed with less emphasis on firearms. According to Creedon's data, approximately half the robberies in Leicestershire and Northamptonshire did not involve a firearm at all.

Two points emerge from this data. The first is that there is no direct relation between the size, the calibre lethality of the weapon and the target chosen. Secondly, there is no discernible relation between the weapon selected and the amount stolen. As noted above, the robbers appear to have little real idea how much money is potentially available (and in some cases do not even get that which is available), while the weapon used tends to be a function of what is available or affordable.

In very few cases in our sample were firearms actually discharged. Indeed they were fired, according to the case notes, in only 6 out of a total of 240 robberies. In three of these incidents they were discharged into the floor or the ceiling in order to frighten cashiers or customers; in two cases shots were fired at the police, injuring an officer on one occasion. In a further case a gun was used to pistol whip a security guard; in another shots were fired at a security van. Both these security van robberies involved amounts in excess of £1 million. In three of the cases in the sample guns were held at the heads of staff or hostages as a threat. Much of the literature on armed robbery makes the point that the more intimidating the weapon the less likely the victim will be to resist and, consequently, there will be fewer injuries. Victims and witnesses, it is argued, are more liable to resist or apprehend the offender if they perceive the robber is vulnerable and lacking firepower. The logic of this argument is that there is little advantage in robbers carrying less firepower since it is likely to lead to a loss of control, to conflict and, ultimately, to injuries (Walsh 1986a; Zimring and Zeuhl 1986). However, the downside of this option is that robberies involving real and loaded firearms are, if used, more likely to result in a serious injury or a fatality. In general, the more powerful the weapon the more likely it is a fatality will result from its use (Cook 1991). It is no doubt the case that the preference of victims, given the choice, between being confronted with a sawn-off shotgun and a handgun would be to opt for the latter.

The police use of weapons

There is a reciprocal relation between the weapons used by the robbers and those used by the police. Quite clearly the choice of weapon is conditioned for both parties by the desire to defend themselves and to contain the perceived threat posed by the other. However, just as the type of weapon used by robbers will be conditioned by other factors besides police activity, so the selection of weapons used by the police to deal with armed robbery is subject to a number of different constraints.

In countries such as Britain in which the public police are defined as 'unarmed', the significance of gun-related crimes is very different from such countries as the USA where the police are routinely armed. However, the notion the British police are 'unarmed' requires some qualification. Our research on the Flying Squad revealed that firearms were regularly distributed amongst its officers. In 1994, for example, the Flying Squad carried out 417 armed operations and was involved in other specialist operations two or three times each week, on average (Matthews 1998). In the course of these operations over the year, 17 shots were fired by armed robbers resulting in six victims sustaining injuries and two others who were fatally wounded. Two police officers also sustained serious injuries. In the course of their operations, the Metropolitan Police appropriated a number of firearms from arrested offenders. In 1994, for example, the Flying Squad recovered 44 handguns, 33 shotguns, 22 pistols, 35 replica guns and 5 air guns.

During the early 1990s a number of high-profile police killings stimulated a national debate on whether the police should be routinely armed (Clarke 1994; Miller 1994). At the time injuries and fatalities suffered by the police were set alongside growing fears about the increased use of violence, particularly associated with the drug trade (Campbell 1994). Media reports suggested guns were becoming more easy to obtain and that criminals were more prepared to use them. In the aftermath of the Brixton riots in the early 1980s there had been a move towards increasing the range of weapons available to the police, including the use of CS gas and new batons. As the number of offences involving firearms increased from 4,750 in 1983 to 8,453 in 1992 and the number of armed police operations in England and Wales increased from 3,180 to 3,722 over the same period, there were repeated calls for the routine arming of the police (Hetherington 1994). The leading advocates for making firearms available to uniformed police officers on the beat were senior police officers and the Police Federation. In a speech given by the Chief Constable of Merseyside at the Association of Chief Police Officers (ACPO) conference in 1994, the Chief Constable is reported to have said:

Firearms incidents are increasing . . . in the past, armed professional criminals would normally be the culprit. Increasingly now it is the young hooligan going into the corner shop, bank and building society. It is the drug dealer seeking to protect territory or turf. There is a wildness about the scene. More sophisticated weapons. We are seeing kalishnikovs, armalites and uzis on a fairly regular basis (Bennetto 1994).

The Chief Constable (who had previously been the chair of the ACPO firearms committee) clearly had a sense of the demise of the old-time professional armed robber and a sense of growing numbers of young 'hooligans' who were becoming involved in commercial robberies, but in raising fears about the importation of more powerful and automatic weapons he fails to make any reference to the trend away from shotguns towards the use of handguns and replicas.

Those who opposed the arming of the police argued it would encourage even first-time offenders to carry firearms. It would also increase the hazards of police work while encouraging the police to resort to firearms more than is strictly necessary. It was suggested that, once the guns were strapped on, it would be very difficult to get rid of them and that it would take us down the US road of a continuing 'arms race' between the police and criminals.

The issue of the routine arming of the police was put to the vote in 1994 and rank-and-file police officers voted four to one against this proposal. This rejection, it has been suggested, was part of a rejection of a wider 'gun culture'. This antipathy towards the more widespread use of firearms was reaffirmed by the national outrage following the killings at Dunblane primary school in March 1996 (Squires 2000). Although there was a general unease about the routine arming of the police there was widespread support in police ranks at the time for the greater use of armed response vehicles (ARVs). However, the response times of ARVs makes them relatively ineffective in reaching the scene of the crime in time to apprehend suspects, particularly in large urban areas. There had also been continuing complaints from police officers that once these vehicles do arrive there are often delays in getting the necessary authorisation to deploy firearms (Waddington 1994; Waddington and Hamilton 1997).

The police have subsequently turned their attention to the possibility of introducing a range of less lethal 'new generation' weaponry, including electrical stun guns, pepper sprays (which temporarily blind the subject), laser guns and glue guns (which emit a sticky foam), bean-bag guns (which fire 'socks' filled with lead shot that knock the subject to the ground) and lasers (which fire probes that can penetrate two inches of clothing before delivering a five-second 5,000 volt electric shock) (Addley 2001).

The control of firearms

The close relation between firearms and commercial robberies that developed during the 1970s and the 1980s in the UK raised the issue of whether the more effective regulation of firearms could serve to reduce the number of armed robberies as well as their impact. Over this period the debate on firearms control became very polarised, with those on one side claiming that controlling the availability of firearms would automatically reduce gun-related crime while those on the other side claimed gun controls are unlikely to have any impact upon gun crime and may in fact exacerbate the problem (Kleck 1997).

The nature of the debate in Britain has been greatly influenced by the ongoing debate in the USA where these issues have taken on a much greater prominence and intensity (Kates and Kleck 1997). Despite the fact that the level of gun ownership and use of the firearms in the USA is exceptional, with approximately 40 per cent of American adults owning a gun (76 million people), the range and relative sophistication of the

American debate on gun control make it an important point of reference and raises a number of issues that are of direct interest to those concerned with exploring the relation between firearms control and armed robbery (Lott 2000).

The initial issue raised in this literature is the connection between the regulation of the legitimate pool of firearms and its impact on gun-related crimes. This question, in turn, raises the question of the relation between legal controls and other forms of regulation. A further issue that arises is the possible substitution effect of different weapons if the availability of some firearms were to be curtailed. Finally, there is a need to consider the relation between different gun control strategies and the level of injuries sustained by victims. In addressing these related questions we will draw on the relevant American literature, bearing in mind it is directed towards a problem that is of a very different scale and intensity from that experienced in most advanced western countries.

An opening foray in the gun control debate in the UK was launched by Colin Greenwood (1972), who argued that attempts to control gun ownership have had little effect on the robbery rate since experienced villains, he claims, can readily obtain firearms, while younger robbers can easily rent or borrow firearms from acquaintances. Alternatively, robbers can use a knife or another type of weapon. Greenwood points out that during the 1950s and 1960s when there were a large number of unregistered guns in circulation (many of which were later confiscated through amnesties), the level of firearm-related robberies was relatively low. It is not therefore, he argues, the number of firearms in circulation that is critical but the size of the illegal pool of firearms. The argument is in part reinforced by the observation there are countries such as Switzerland in which firearms are widely available but that experience a relatively low level of gun crime. This observation is encapsulated in the slogan: 'Its not guns that kill people – people kill people.' It is therefore not the availability of guns that is important but the nature of the 'gun culture' itself that is critical in determining the level of gun crime (Zimring and Hawkins 1997).

There are a number of flaws in this argument. First, there is a symbiotic relationship between the availability of firearms and the expansion of a 'gun culture'. As Tom Diaz (1999) has pointed out, guns are aggressively marketed in the USA and the manufacturers and distributors of guns have a vested interest in actively promoting this multimillion dollar business. Secondly, without guns the ability of people to kill people would be radically diminished. Thirdly, guns have an 'instumentality effect', by which is meant the objective dangerousness of a weapon used in violent attacks appears to be an another determinant of the number of victims who die from these attacks (Cook 1991). Thus in the USA it has been estimated that the death rate from gun robbery nationwide is four times that of non-gun robberies (Zimring and Hawkins 1997). The fourth limitation in this proposition is that all guns begin their lives as legitimate weapons. What is important is how and when (and in what quantities) they make the transitions into the illegal pool of firearms. Significantly, it is estimated that about a thousand guns a year are stolen from certificate holders in the UK (Squires 2000).

Thus, central to the debate in Britain is the size, composition and location of the illegal pool of firearms since these factors will determine how easily those engaging in such crimes as armed robbery will be able to acquire firearms. The guestimates are that there are in the region of one million unregistered firearms in the UK. However, there are a number of reasons for believing this figure is widely exaggerated and that the availability of illegal firearms may be much more restricted than is generally assumed. The first arises from the responses given by the convicted armed robbers whom we interviewed and from related research. We were told by a number of interviewees that if you are not 'connected' you would find it very difficult and probably dangerous to attempt to purchase a gun illegally. This suggests that guns are not readily available and that to get hold of real firearms involves having some credibility amongst the criminal fraternity. This restricted availability, particularly to those who have not established criminal contacts and credentials, has been demonstrated by journalists who have tried to purchase guns in the UK (Mungo 1996).[1]

A further proposition that has appeared in the literature alongside the slogan 'guns don't kill people – people kill people' is that if there were more guns there would be less crime (Lott 2000). The basis of this contention is that if more people have guns then criminals would be less likely to use guns for fear of retaliation, while law-abiding citizens would be able effectively to protect themselves against gun-toting predators (Wilson 1994). While this proposition may have some currency in the USA where guns are widely available, from a British vantage point the claim 'more guns equals less crime' appears bizarre and perverse. The obvious consequence of cashiers, security staff and customers being routinely armed would be to escalate the level of gun use – with robbers having to carry real and loaded weapons – with the result that real guns would increasingly become a normal part of commercial robberies. There would be more accidents and more impulsive killings and a drift towards the use of maximum force. Moreover, Lott (2000) admits that, in the USA where armed guards are already present in most commercial establishments, the carrying of guns by the public would be of little advantage.

If it is the case that the overall objective of gun control is to decrease the level and impact of gun crime, the issue remains of the most effective way to regulate firearms in Britain. Because the tragedies that occurred in Hungerford in 1987 and in Dunblane in 1996 were both committed by persons holding firearms certificates there has been considerable pressure to outlaw the ownership of guns. Legislation, in the form of the Firearms (Amendment) Act 1988, prohibited the acquisition of semi-automatic rifles, burst-firing weapons and pump-action shotguns. The Firearms (Amendment) Act 1997 banned the private ownership of virtually all handguns and resulted in the removal of some 162,000 handguns from the private collections of gun owners (National Audit Office 1999). It is generally considered this legislation has been much more effective than the various attempts to control guns in the USA through licensing and other legislative measures, which are held to be relatively ineffectual (Kleck 1991; Diaz 1999). The difference in the effectiveness of legalisation in both Britain and the USA also appears to be bound up with differences in the two countries' gun cultures, together with differences in public tolerance and attitudes towards firearms.

Thus, formal legal controls appear to have benefited from changes in public sensibilities such that there has been a shift in attitudes towards interpersonal violence in Britain, while carrying a gun is not seen as necessary for self-defence or as an essential for the maintenance of individual rights. As such, over the last two decades a process of 'civilian disarmament' has been enacted in the UK that has almost certainly had a depressing effect on firearms-related crime. Although the number of crimes involving firearms increased up to 1993, it seems highly probable that without legislative controls it would have been significantly higher. As Peter Squires (2000) argues, the liberalising of the present legislation would appear to be a backward step and that it is clear that the adaptation of universal gun laws in the USA has not been accompanied by low rates in gun crime. On the contrary, the types of urban gun laws in operation in the USA provide a continual reminder of the dangers of liberalism and individualism while providing a continuing negative point of reference in the gun control debate. Apart from the legal control of firearms, there have been a number of complementary strategies designed to reduce the pool of illegal firearms in the UK, including amnesties, import control and the regulation of the reactivation of guns.

There have been a number of gun amnesties in recent years during which a surprisingly high number of unregistered firearms have been handed in. One amnesty that was introduced following the Hungerford shooting in 1987 gathered up approximately 48,000 weapons. Although it is largely recognised that such amnesties have little direct impact on the level of gun crime, they do help to drain the pool of unregistered weapons.

Apart from amnesties there has been an ongoing effort to limit the importation of illegal firearms by customs officials. During the 1990s there were a number of reports of firearms being illegally shipped from abroad, particularly from Eastern Europe. Each year Customs & Excise confiscate a number of firearms. In 1997, 333 handguns, 174 rifles and 362 shotguns were seized (Customs & Excise 1997).[2] There are also some weapons that enter the country that have been diverted from the legal trade. However, keeping track of these weapons is difficult because there is no internationally agreed and effective system of marking weapons (Cukier and Shropshire 2000).

Most firearms used in armed robberies have probably been recycled. There is evidence in the UK of thriving local cottage industries specialising in the recycling of deactivated weapons (Bryan 1999). Also, there appears to be a growing number of replica and imitation firearms used in 'armed' robberies (Morrison and O'Donnell 1994). The increasingly authentic appearance of replica firearms makes it difficult for victims or witnesses of robberies to distinguish them from real firearms. The ready availability and low cost of these weapons make them particularly attractive to certain groups of commercial robbers. Consequently there have been calls for the prohibition of replica guns in order to reduce the number of robberies and related crimes, although concerns have been expressed that this might encourage prospective robbers to substitute other weapons with greater lethality, such as knives or even real firearms (Taylor and Hornsby 2000). However, allowing the increased distribution of replicas, it is argued, puts the user at risk because the police have to assume the gun is real even though it may not be. It also strengthens arguments for the police to be routinely armed in order that they can respond to a growing number of 'firearm' incidents (Fry 198, 1991).

In sum, gun control measures in England and Wales do appear to have had a significant impact, not only through legislation that has restricted the number of firearms in general circulation but also through the 'educative' effect of legislation. These legal controls – coupled with a range of other strategies including amnesties and the like – have almost certainly reduced the pool of illegal weapons. It is also evident from interviews with convicted armed robbers that there is an ambivalence in relation to firearms and that, because of the cost and time involved as well as the desire not to engage in unnecessary violence, many prefer less lethal weapons, such as replicas. The issue now is whether these replicas constitute a new problem and need to be controlled in the ways in which real firearms have been regulated in the past, or whether such controls would encourage armed robbers to deploy weapons with greater lethality.[3]

Sentencing armed robbers

As the proportion of commercial robberies involving the use of replicas and imitation and implied firearms increases, the meaning of the term 'armed' is becoming uncertain. These uncertainties create, in theory at least, a number of problems for developing an equitable and effective sentencing policy.

Sentencing policy in England and Wales has, for many years, deployed a mixture of retribution, deterrence (both general and specific), incapacitation and rehabilitation to deal with those convicted of armed robbery. That is, convicted robbers have been sentenced in response to the perceived harm inflicted on victims and to deter them and other potential robbers from engaging in this offence, taking them out of circulation for relatively long periods of time and, in some cases, anticipating that prisons will provide courses and training that will reduce the desire to commit robberies. The net result of this combination of rationales is that over 90 per cent of convicted armed robbers in England and Wales receive a prison sentence, while the average prison sentence is 6.6 years (Morrison and O'Donnell, 1994).

Arguably, this sentencing policy has been developed around a fairly undifferentiated conception of 'armed robbery' and is concerned primarily with reducing the overall level of commercial robbery rather than aiming to reduce the threat and trauma to victims and witnesses. Developing a sentencing policy that prioritises the latter objective would provide a response that sentenced offenders in terms of the actual threat posed, the degree of violence expressed and the potential lethality of the weapon used. Thus a rational sentencing policy that aims to minimise actual or possible threats to staff, to members of the public or to the police would adopt a policy of 'selective' deterrence that reserves the most severe punishments for those involved in life-threatening activities rather than a general deterrence that applies severe punishments to virtually all, irrespective of the type of weapon used and its potential impact.

As the law stands in England and Wales there is very little disincentive for armed robbers to carry unloaded or imitation weapons since the sentence they will receive will be roughly similar, other things being equal. This policy is justified on the basis of the immediate trauma of the victim, who is often unable to tell whether a real gun is involved and whether it is loaded or not. Such a justification is, however, short sighted and ultimately counterproductive since if no distinction is made between the robber who carries a loaded firearm and one who carries an imitation, there is little effective disincentive for robbers not to carry loaded firearms, thus posing a risk in future robberies to potential victims. An undifferentiated sentencing policy that makes little or no distinction between the different types of weapons involved fails to recognise that a gun which is loaded constitutes a lethal weapon, a firearm which is unloaded is a piece of metal and a courgette is a vegetable.

As Philip Cook (1987: 370–71) has pointed out in relation to American sentencing policy, there has been some movement in recent years towards a more differentiated approach based on the 'objective dangerousness' of the weapons used in criminal activities:

> [In particular] armed robbery is subject to more severe punishment than unarmed, 'strong-arm' robbery. A number of States have recently delineated a further distinction between armed robbery and unarmed robbery. A survey of 900 assistant prosecutors found that they perceived gun robbery as substantially more serious than robbery with a blunt object or with physical force. One argument in favour of such weapons-based distinctions derives from the notion of 'objective dangerousness': that the likelihood of serious injury and death in robbery is influenced *inter alia* by the type of weapon employed by the assailant. Hence the seriousness of a robbery is associated with weapon type regardless of outcome.

Similarly, in terms of incapacitation, a rational sentencing policy would devise selective policies if the aim is to reduce violent crime. Research on incapacitation suggests that long-term detention is effective for only a limited number of offenders and that, as a general strategy, incapacitation provides a limited but nevertheless extremely costly sentencing strategy (Zimring and Hawkins 1997). Thus:

> Some current policies do not seem coherent even on the basis of the limited data currently available. Assigning equivalent punishment to robbers with toy guns and robbers with real ones makes sense only if property interests are more important than human bodily integrity. Across-the-board increases in penal sanctions blur the distinction between life threatening and other offences. Incomplete as current information may be, the prevention of life threatening violence is yet another aspect of the criminal justice system where we know better than we do (ibid.: 184).

There is, as we have seen, an ambivalence amongst armed robbers in relation to the use of firearms. A rational sentencing policy would exploit this ambivalence and give robbers every incentive to carry the least objectively dangerous and lethal weapons available.

Conclusion

The term 'armed robbery' needs to be deconstructed carefully. Many so-called armed robberies involve other weapons besides firearms, and the 'firearms' used in a significant percentage of cases are not capable of firing a lethal shot. There is also evidence that indicates that commercial robberies, in London at least, are increasingly carried out by assailants who have no weapon at all but who simply bluff it or, alternatively, engage in 'steaming' whereby a gang runs into the premises, creates mayhem and intimidates the staff, jumps over the counter and steals the money from the till. The apparent growth of these 'armed robberies' in which the offenders are actually unarmed may be a function of the difficulties and cost of acquiring real firearms. It may also be because there is a desire not to cause serious or fatal injuries. The available evidence, although patchy, suggests that the availability of illegal firearms in the UK is limited and that those who do not have the right contacts may well find it difficult to acquire a proper working firearm. If this observation is correct it suggests the gun control policy that has been developed over the last decade or so is working reasonably well and that the emerging issue now is over the desirability of controlling the production and distribution of replicas.

For those who choose to use real firearms there has been a clear shift in recent years away from shotguns and towards handguns, and this change coincides with a decrease in attacks on banks and building societies. This change, however, has arisen not because there is a direct relation between weapon choice and the target selected but, largely, because shotguns are increasingly seen as cumbersome and unfashionable and the preference amongst the new generation of commercial robbers is for a weapon that is smarter, more easy to conceal and easier to use.

Notes

1 Apparently, a *News of the World* reporter claimed he bought nine illegal firearms in one day. However, the reporter had apparently spent months setting up these deals and had to pay an inflated price for the guns. Rather than demonstrate the

ease of obtaining guns (which the article set out to do), it inadvertently showed how difficult it is in the UK to acquire working firearms (see Mungo 1996).

2   The Home Affairs Committee (2000) reported that 'the Government believes that the widespread use of reactivated firearms in organised crime is evidence that, despite the wide availability of "conventional weaponry" on the Continent, few weapons are being smuggled into the country.'

3   In the USA there have been a succession of municipal and federal laws enacted requiring all toy guns to feature brightly coloured markings to distinguish them from real weapons (see Taylor and Hornsby 2000).

Chapter 5

Victims of robbery

Introduction

One of the most noticeable developments in recent years has been the growing focus on the victims of crime. The rise of the victim's movement, the growth of organisations such as Victim's Support and other specialist agencies designed to assist the victims of crime have served increasingly to bring victims into the centre of criminological inquiry. Given these developments it is remarkable how little research and information is available on the victims of armed robbery, which is arguably one of the most serious and traumatic forms of criminal victimisation. Of the limited number of studies that have been conducted, very few are by independent researchers and most of the research on the victims of armed robbery has been carried out 'in-house' by the larger financial and commercial organisations who are generally unwilling to make their findings publicly available. There is some quantitative material that has been produced using *British Crime Survey* data on the distribution of commercial victimisation (Mirrlees-Black and Ross 1995), and a slightly more specialist overview of the victimisation of retail outlets (notably shops, garages, off-licences, convenience stores and the like) is provided in a series of reports published by the British Retail Consortium (Brooks and Cross 1996; BRS 1999). The Health and Safety Executive (HSE) has published a number of reports that examine the issue of violence at work more generally, as well as specific guidelines on the prevention of violence to staff working in banks and building societies (HSE 1993; Standing and Nicolini 1997; Poyner *et al* 2000).

Although the available data is patchy, this chapter draws on these various sources in order to examine the experience, impact, dynamics and distribution of robbery victimisation. It also draws on the interviews that were conducted with convicted armed robbers in order to investigate the processes of victim selection and to elicit robbers' attitudes towards victims. The distribution of armed robberies is examined in some detail through an analysis of the data supplied by the Metropolitan Police, which covers all Band 1 robberies in the London area over a three-year period (1992–94). Thus, this chapter is divided between an examination of the victimisation of individuals and the victimisation of businesses and organisations. There is, however, a necessary overlap between these two forms of victimisation but it is important when looking at robbery victimisation to keep in mind the relative autonomy of personal and institutional victimisation since what may be seen as being 'serious' for one may be considered unimportant for the other. It is also the case, as we shall see, that attempts to reduce victimisation in one form can promote victimisation in another.

Violence at work

Research has shown there has been a gradual increase over the last decade in work-related violence (Mirrlees-Black 1988). According to the *British Crime Survey*, there were 770,000 incidents in 1995. Those most at risk from physical violence were welfare workers, nurses, police managers, security guards and retailers. Others at risk are staff in fast-food outlets, bars and off-licences. According to the 1992 *British Crime Survey* almost half work-related incidents occur between 6 p.m. and midnight. One per cent of working adults reported being a victim of physical attacks at work in 1999, and security personal, cashiers and retail staff were amongst those who saw themselves as most likely to experience violence at work (Budd 1999).

In the USA, workplace violence is also prevalent. Between 1992–1996, an average of 330,000 retail employees were victimised and about 84,000 employees nationally were robbed in the workplace. Between 1994 and 1996, however, violence in the workplace decreased by just over 20 per cent. Police officers and prison warders were the two groups who most frequently report workplace violence. However private security guards, retail staff, station attendants and those working in convenience and liquor stores also reported a relatively high level of workplace victimisation (Warchol 1998).

In 1988 Barry Poyner and Caroline Warne provided a framework for examining violence in the workplace, which was designed to be used as a basis for assessment and prevention. According to their model, an understanding of violent incidents requires a focus on five basic elements:

the assailant, the employee, the type of interaction, the situation and the outcome. In relation to the assailant, they see the critical determinants as personality type and expectations. Employees are distinguished in terms of health, appearance, temperament and gender. Whether the employee is in a caring, educational, controlling or service occupation is seen as an important component, as is whether he or she is working alone. The location of the job is held to influence outcomes and they distinguish between outcomes that involve physical and verbal abuse and those that involve threats with a weapon and attempted injury.

Poyner and Warne's (1988) model has been 'enriched' by Standing and Nicolini (1997), who suggest that a better understanding of workplace violence can be gained from shifting the focus from the individual assailant/victim towards the organisational context. In addition, there is a need, Standing and Nicolini argue, to distinguish more clearly between different types of violence. Thus although Poyner and Warne's model is credited with including some consideration of the situation and the context in which workplace violence occurs, this is an essentially individualistic and interpersonal model that focuses on the interactional aspects of the incident as determined by the characteristics of offenders and victims. Emphasising the organisational and contextual framework in which workplace violence occurs, Standing and Nicolini argue, moves away from seeing these as random events and to seeing them instead as patterned and predictable. Secondly, in contrast to the linear model represented by Poyner and Warne, a broader perspective can incorporate the wider social and organisational processes that influence and shape the perpetration of violence and the responses to it. In this way, it is argued, it is possible to develop preventative strategies at the organisational level. Importantly, Standing and Nicolini emphasise that this organisational perspective allows for a distinction between the roles of the organisation and the employee in relation to the occurrence of violence.

While the emphasis on a broader organisational perspective is to be welcomed, Standing and Nicolini's (1997) approach is, ultimately, as managerialist and mechanical as that presented by Poyner and Warne (1988). They demonstrate little understanding of the negotiated and contingent aspects of robbery or much appreciation of the differential impact of work-related violence on individual victims. Consequently, they are unable to delineate the appropriateness of different crime reduction strategies on the security and well-being of staff. The problems with this managerialist approach are that it assumes a consensus of interest between the managers and owners of different organisations and their employees, and it fails to appreciate fully that violence reduction programmes are not uncontested issues but ultimately involve considerations of rights and responsibilities. Rather than engage with these complex issues they predictably call for more research, improved forms of data collection and the development of 'good practice'.

In a publication by the Health and Safety Executive on *Prevention of Violence to Staff in Banks and Building Societies* (HSE 1993), it was pointed out that employers have a legal duty to protect, so far as is reasonably practicable, the health and safety of employees, and this includes the need to deal with the risk of violence at work from criminals. As guidance to employers, the HSE sets out an 'integrated policy' involving a risk management process, education and training programmes, a post-robbery support system and a public relations strategy in order to minimise intrusion into the privacy of staff and to protect the integrity of security procedures. The report provides a useful overview of some of the strategies that can be developed by banks and building societies to deal with armed robbery. However, there is no indication that banks and building societies have changed their practices following the publication of this report. As we shall see, the limited evidence available suggests that the protection given to staff by some of the larger companies falls a long way short of the HSE's guidelines. It is indicative, however, that since the publication of the report in 1993 there has not been a single prosecution of a bank or building society under the Health and Safety at Work Act 1974.

In a recent commentary on work-related violence, Poyner *et al* (2000) explore the issue of violence at work through a number of case studies that include a number of different types of commercial premises. In their report they point to the limitations of mechanistic and managerialist approaches by arguing that dealing with violence at work is not so much an issue of cost-effectiveness or risk management but requires instead the provision of more thought and care. Some of the most effective measures, they argue, are social and informal, such as avoiding eye contact or dropping to the floor when threatened. They point out that security equipment is issued primarily for securing the premises when unoccupied rather than reducing violence to staff. In small and medium-sized business they suggest the human factor is important and that dealing effectively with threats of violence is often a function of the interpersonal skills of the cashier. Similarly, they argue, risks are variable, and dealing with robberies and violent attacks is not subject to a formalised managerialist approach but is likely to require a range of different responses. Also they note that the type of procedures for information gathering and monitoring suggested in previous HSE reports are likely to be too time consuming and generally inappropriate for small businesses. Although this report could be criticised for offering an essentially individualistic account that places more responsibility on the employee rather than the employer, it is no doubt correct in identifying some of the limitations of managerialism and in emphasising the negotiated aspects of the victim–offender encounter.

The selection of victims

Just as we have shown that it is not very helpful, either conceptually or practically, to try to explain the robber's selection of targets in terms of a crude rational/irrational dichotomy, so the process of victim selection cannot be adequately explained in such terms. In many cases the selection of victims – whether a cashier, shop assistant or security guard – may be prestructured and subject to a range of situational and contextual determinants over which the robber has no control and therefore is able to exercise little or no choice. This is not to say that the selection of personal victims is random or totally arbitrary. Rather, it is to suggest that the range of choice available to the commercial robber in relation to the selection of victims is highly structured and circumscribed. At the same time it is influenced by a number of contingencies and is often guided by hunches, prejudices and intuitions as well as other 'irrational' considerations. In examining the accounts given by robbers about the selection of victims, we find a number of statements to the effect they were acting on impulse or intuition or, in some cases, that they had little awareness of the type of victim they were likely to confront. As robbers tried to account retrospectively for their selection of victims, they expressed a deep ambivalence regarding victims, which oscillated between sympathy and sensitivity at one moment to vindictiveness at another.

Many robbers who were interviewed in prison expressed concern and sympathy for their victims and pointed out they went to considerable lengths to avoid injuries to children, elderly people and others whom they considered 'undeserving' victims. Not all robbers, however, endorsed this viewpoint and they took the position that people who work in financial institutions or retail outlets know the risks when they take on the job and that if they cannot deal with these situations, they should choose another type of job.

As Dermot Walsh (1986b) admits in his discussions of victim selection, robbers will often refrain from a robbery because it does not 'feel right' (or for some other intangible reason). In recognising that explanations in terms of 'rationality' are not enough, Walsh points to the role of luck and fatalism in influencing decisions. Within this complex framework, the decision-making and selection rationality attributed to the offender may well be a gloss imposed by the researcher after the event rather than an accurate depiction of the decision-making process engaged in by the offender.

That which does not fit neatly into the box of 'rational decision-making' is too easily dismissed by researchers, despite the fact that 'non-rational' responses may be more important to the process. It may well also be the case that by focusing on the most 'obvious' components of decision-making we overlook the more subtle and complex processes at work. There is also a tendency to conflate the perceived decision-making processes engaged in by 'planners' and professionals with the more disorganised 'amateurs'.

A familiar theme that emerged from both 'planners' and 'amateurs' alike was that there was no a priori intention or desire physically to hurt the employees in the premises they robbed. For the majority, engaging in violence is seen only as legitimate in cases where the cashier/sales person or security guard refuses to co-operate or attempts actively to resist the attack. Demonstrations of force are also seen as legitimate if it is felt to be necessary to gain compliance. Normally such force takes the form of threats, verbal gestures or the presentation of a weapon. In a few cases robbers fired shots into the floor or the ceiling. Alternatively, they put a gun to the head of the victim. Non-compliance may be responded to with the victim being hit with a weapon or pushed around. Serious violence is normally reserved for 'have-a-go heroes' and those who adamantly refuse to comply with the robbers' demands, despite repeated threats.

The critical point of the robbery can occur when the initial demand is met with non-compliance (Luckenbill 1980, 1981). For both the robber and the victim, this moment heightens the tensions and uncertainties and creates a situation in which either the level of threat or violence will increase or, alternatively, the robber will withdraw. A considerable percentage of the robbers we interviewed candidly admitted that, if they met with non-compliance, they would make a hasty retreat. However, for others such a response was seen to require an immediate escalation in the level of threat issued, but the difficult problem for the robber is to what degree the threat or violence needs to be increased to overcome resistance. Too much gratuitous violence or verbal abuse may signal a loss of control or vulnerability on the part of the robber. Too little, on the other hand, may make the robber appear light-weight and unconvincing. In one robbery on a building society in central London, in which the robber's demands were met with non-compliance, the course of the robbery took a not unfamiliar turn:

I went back into the building society at about quarter past one, during the lunch hour when there was less staff than there would normally be in. I just went up to one and handed a note over the counter which said: 'PASS ALL THE MONEY OVER THE COUNTER.' It was written in block capitals and the teller read the note and instead of handing over the money, which is the normal practice – or had been the normal practice when I have handed notes over in the past, and I had robbed this branch before I was in prison, from where I had escaped and I was now on the run robbing the branch again. There had been no trouble with this building society at all so she should have just handed over the money and that's it. I could have just walked out but this particular time she didn't do anything, so I urged her on, got a bit more aggressive and took a knife out of the briefcase that I had on the counter and instead of handing me the money over and becoming more frightened she was determined not to give me any more money and instead of going to the till drawer she went for a button somewhere below the till and the blinds came flying up from the top of the desk and this completely cut me off from the banking sector. I was quite shocked but I had enough rationality about me to pick up my briefcase and walk out.

Even more critical for the robber is when the victim or a bystander decides to react physically. Such a response threatens the very logic of the robbery and, most importantly, undermines the key objective of gaining and maintaining control. It forces the robber either immediately to increase the level of violence or to face the danger of being overcome and caught.

There is, moreover, a real possibility the offender turns victim. In a number of cases in our sample, robbers inflicted quite serious injuries on themselves either in the course of the robbery or in the attempt to escape. Receiving cuts and wounds from flying glass was reported in two cases, while others reported hurting themselves climbing across the counter or when trapped by rising screens. There were also cases in which serious injuries were sustained by robbers as a result of police intervention.

As much as robbers exercised a degree of choice in the selection of victims, it was evident they gravitated in most cases towards what they considered the more vulnerable and compliant victims. It also became apparent that these conceptions of the effects of their actions were at odds with the actual experience of the victims themselves (Morrison 1993).

The experience and impact of armed robbery

All the available evidence indicates that the level of physical injury sustained in commercial robberies is surprisingly low, while the degree of trauma suffered by victims can be extremely high and long lasting. Within our Metropolitan Police sample of 240 cases some 5 per cent involved some form of physical injury requiring medical treatment, 9 per cent involved a physical threat or assault and over 70 per cent involved the presentation of a firearm, whether real or imitation. In nine cases a firearm was discharged.

Research carried out in Montreal found that those resisting offenders were ten times more likely to sustain injuries (Gabor *et al* 1987). In this study it was found that over 90 per cent of victims had experienced an increase in fear, distrust, aggressiveness, mood swings and depression following a robbery. In over 80 per cent of these cases victims were still displaying symptoms 6 months after the robbery and about 20 per cent recorded changes in their social life and indicated that one effect of victimisation was a significant change of lifestyle. The available evidence strongly suggests there is a considerable difference between the reality of an armed robbery for many victims and the way it is presented in training manuals or portrayed in the media. As one victim of armed robbery reports: 'You don't release your eyes off the gun: it's not like you think it would be, not like on television. I've never been so frightened. It's panic...I can't even talk about it now without shaking (Grant 1992).

This victim was beaten unconscious. Nevertheless, she returned to work after two weeks although she did not think she had recovered properly. This case signifies the extreme violence and trauma suffered by some victims who are encouraged by their employers to play down the effects of the robbery and to return to work. In some cases victims can experience the effects of the robbery for months and even years after the event, while others may leave their job without proper compensation to try to find less hazardous work.

One research study carried out in the branches of two high-street banks (involving a sample of 75 employees who had experienced armed robberies between 1994 and 1997) found that although the majority had only been involved in one raid, some had experienced two robberies and two had experienced three robberies over this period (Bains and Richards 1998). It was found that of the 32 raids in the sample violence was threatened in 25 raids, but very rarely carried out and no staff suffered physical injury. The most common weapon carried was a handgun (14 raids), with shotguns carried four times and knives in two raids. In 12 raids no weapon was seen. Firearms were discharged in only two raids. Damage to property occurred on five occasions – consisting of gun-shot damage in two raids and smashed glass, smashed doors and forced locks in three others. Indicatively, only three out of four of these raids resulted in financial loss and, in 24 raids, the loss to the bank was less than £3,000 on each occasion.

These robberies resulted in an increase in the overall sickness rates in the six-month period following the robbery as a result of psychological stress (Richards 2000). The main symptoms were found to be stress, anxiety and depression, as well as health problems. Employees also reported experiencing sleep disturbance, increased irritability and fearfulness, poor concentration and mood swings. While most employees appear to recover from these incidents fairly quickly, for others the symptoms persist for weeks and even months and may develop into a form of post-traumatic stress disorder (PTSD). Most employees reported they were unprepared for the reality of the raid and that training was poor. Post-robbery support was also found to be patchy and limited. One of the banks provided little organisational and managerial support, while the other provided a more elaborate range of services and supports for individual victims. In some branches managers simply instructed employees to carry on after the robbery as if nothing had happened. Most banks provide debriefing sessions for employees who have experienced a robbery, but responses to these sessions were mixed amongst employees working at both banks, with some finding them useful while others were less impressed. The system of financial compensation employed by banks was generally seen as inadequate. The amounts paid out to staff were variable and some staff felt undervalued. As one employee put it: 'Is £200 all I am worth?' Thus:

Of all those available to give support in the aftermath of the raid, employees' colleagues were rated most highly, even when employees had to move to branches where no-one else had been involved in the raid. When managers gave good support they were seen as extremely supportive and helpful. Unfortunately, managers' responses to raids and raided employees varied wildly, with some managers making employees wish that they could leave their jobs. Support from management appeared to be a product of individual managers' sensitivity coupled with a perception that if someone made an assessment that the raid was 'bad', more care would be lavished on employees (Bains and Richards 1998: 17).

It is evident from this research that the support given to staff (even by wealthy financial institutions) is uneven and in many key respects, open to criticism. For the growing number of individual victims in shops, garages, off-licences and other premises owned by less wealthy and less established commercial organisations, the levels of organisational support are in many cases likely to be minimal. It is also the case that in some of these robberies the perpetrators are more desperate, disorganised and unpredictable than those carrying out raids against banks.

The experiences of robbery victims in the UK is similar to that found in other parts of the world. A recent report from Australia, for example, found that most commercial organisations and managers display a lack of recognition of the length of trauma experienced by some victims. The support provided tends to be inappropriate, relying on medication (mainly in the form of tranquillisers). Cashiers and store staff are not generally prepared psychologically for the impact of the robbery and are rarely trained in identifying robbers (Leeman-Conley 1990). In the USA, an organisation called Transitions and Trauma, which specialises in giving advice on dealing with the effects of bank robberies, offers what it calls a 'positive response programme' to employers, but makes it clear that this response is 'Not therapeutic, but rather focuses on working to stabilize the work environment so that people are able to resume effectiveness' (Transitions and Trauma 2001). That is, they are only interested in the well-being of staff who have been victims of robbery to the extent that it affects their ability to carry out their jobs effectively and efficiently.

The general difficulties victims confront when attempting to identify offenders have been well documented (Kebbell and Wagstaff 1999). Paradoxically, however, the intensity of the experience and the presence of a weapon can serve to focus the mind and to concentrate attention towards the incident itself and away from peripheral information. Victims of serious crimes, it has been found, can sometimes maintain accurate memories of an offence over a long period of time, particularly in cases where they repeatedly go over the event in their minds. Research has found that, generally, witnesses are more accurate with their descriptions of certain offender characteristics (such as sex, hair colour and distinguishing features) than others (such as height and race). It is also important to note that some witnesses may be uncertain about the description of suspects but accurate and confident on identification.

Post-robbery support comes in a number of different forms – emotional support (listening and reassurance), psychological support (counselling), information support (advice and information on available services) and institutional support (compensation, money, time off). Effective post-robbery support will necessarily involve a combination of these responses. In Heinz Leymann's (1990) study of the support offered to victims of armed robbery in Sweden, he found that a significant percentage of employees complained that management had taken little or no interest in their experience as victims and that where visits and contacts were made, they were often token and short lived. In terms of the police response, many found their treatment by the police to be insensitive and generally unpleasant, and about one third of victims complained they received no information about whether the offender was caught, prosecuted or convicted.

It would be wrong to characterise all victims as passive and powerless. Victims can, and do, resist. Often for reasons that seem inexplicable to armed robbers, victims refuse to co-operate. Victim resistance, it would seem, however, is not driven by any discernible 'rationality' or even simply by fear. Other processes are involved. As Thomas Gabor (1987: 105) and his colleagues found, the motivations that guide victim resistance do not appear to involve a process of rational decision-making:

On the whole much of the information we have accumulated on resistance suggests the frequent absence of sound reasoning on the victim's part. Aside from the apparent unimportance of the number of witnesses present, victims on the whole did not take into account the number of offenders present, nor their own position in the store. Rather resistance was often motivated by anger, related to threats and even prior experiences. Furthermore, there was usually a consistency in the victim's behaviour from the beginning to the end of the armed robbery. Such a consistency may reflect an underlying inclination to react in a certain way, rather than to act upon a continuous reappraisal of what is actually a fluid event.

Gender, race and victimisation

The issues of gender and race take on a prominence when examining the victims of armed robbery, since many of the larger financial institutions employ a high proportion of women, while a considerable number of shops and businesses in the UK are run by Asians and other ethnic minority groups.

It was also evident in our interviews with armed robbers that gender and race considerations influenced the selection of victims, and this was related to perceived differences in victim resistance. There was found to be a preference for female victims, particularly amongst those robbers working alone. Similar findings have been presented by American researchers (Zimring and Zeuhl 1986). The expectation is that female staff are less likely to offer resistance and to be more compliant. The following is from a typical interview with an offender who robbed a building society:

We just felt about for premises which looked quite easy – mainly women in the office. They don't seem to give you much hassle.

From a coward's point of view they're the weaker sex and they don't seem to have a go. They seem to be terrified more than men.

Although not all admitted they sought out female cashiers, no respondents said they actively sought out male staff. The only exceptions were a few robbers who sought out young cashiers of either gender whom, they felt, looked vulnerable.

Thus although there was a clear preference for female victims, this view was by no means universal. Some robbers felt female cashiers could be difficult, might freeze or could become hysterical. Either way, such responses were seen as a possible impediment to the overall success of the robbery. Interestingly, despite the views of the majority of robbers that women were more likely to comply with their demands, a significant percentage of the reported robberies that had failed involved female cashiers. Either they simply refused to hand over the money, dropped to the floor or activated rising screens or alarms.

Just as some robbers operated with notions of 'suitable' victims based on more or less accurate gender stereotypes, so others operated with identifiable racial stereotypes. The most common racial stereotype held by the robbers who were interviewed in prison was that Asian shopkeepers were unsuitable victims because they were likely to be owners or related to the owners of the establishment and, therefore, less likely to be willing to part with the money. In one case where an offender decided not to rob a shop owned and run by an Indian family, the offender said: 'So I had a look and all that and I know that these Paki's ain't going to give the money out. I know that for a fact.'

Research, however, has shown that some 17 per cent of Asian-run newsagents and grocery stores in London have been robbed at some time, with 67 per cent of these respondents claiming they had been robbed over the last year (Ekblom and Simon 1988). There were, however, found to be considerable differences in the number of raids against Asian-run shops in different parts of London, with only 6 per cent of the newsagents and grocery shops in Muswell Hill experiencing a robbery compared to 34 per cent in Brixton, 9 per cent in Brent and 14 per cent in Newham reporting they had experienced a robbery in the past. Indicatively, while 7 per cent of white shopkeepers sampled in Brixton had been victims of robbery, only 3 per cent of black shopkeepers reported experiencing a robbery. To what extent these differences in the victimisation of different ethnic groups are a function of demographics, types of premises or levels of security remains unclear. Unfortunately, the available research does not allow the clear identification of the causal relations involved.

The research carried out on race and robbery in the UK has largely ignored the effects of the victim's race on the police responses, the success and failure rates of robberies and the levels of protection and support given to staff. There is also little research on the racial differences between victims and offenders (Cohen *et al* 1981; Cook 1990; Hibberd and Shapland 1993; Bachman, 1996).[1]

The distribution of commercial robberies

In 1993, 4 per cent of retailers experienced one or more robberies or attempted robberies (Speed *et al* 1995). These robberies were concentrated amongst certain types of retail premises, with those selling alcohol and cigarettes located in quiet streets away from the main shopping areas being the main targets. Those operating extended opening hours (particularly those open late at night) experienced considerably higher rates of victimisation. Significant regional differences have also been noted in relation to robberies against retail premises, with the greatest concentration occurring in London and the north west. The loss from robbers and till snatches constituted 2 per cent of the total losses arising from crime against retail premises in 1994–95 and involved an estimated £29 million. This compares to losses of £446 million resulting from staff theft and £664 million resulting from customer theft (Brooks and Cross 1996). The average loss per robbery incident in 1994–95 was £1,288, but this figure was inflated by a number of robberies from jewellers where the loss averaged around £30,000.

Although robberies and till snatches involve a relatively small percentage of crimes committed against retail premises, their significance is increased because of the use or threat of violence. Retailers reported that just over 12,000 staff were subjected to physical violence in 1993–94. Another 90,000 staff were subjected to threats of violence and another 209,000 were victims of verbal abuse. The 1993–94 *Retail Crime Survey* found that nearly 20 per cent of these attacks arose in relation to robberies. The risk of physical violence was found to be highest in off-licences. Overall, however, it is important to note that the number of retail staff suffering physical violence decreased by 50 per cent between 1993 and 1995.

The British Retail Consortium's response to the problem of violence against staff has been to advocate increased training so as to equip retail staff with the skills to deal with the issue of violence. There is, however, no discussion of employer's responsibilities and liabilities in this respect or the need to develop more effective support, counselling or compensation programmes.

The 1999 *Retail Crime Survey* noted a continued decrease in the number of robberies experienced in retail outlets, down to 1 per cent of recorded crimes and amounting to losses of £15 million from robberies and till snatches. The robbery risk rate for independent stores decreased from 20 per 100 outlets in 1998 to 6 per 100 outlets in 1999, while the cost of robbery to independent retailers also decreased dramatically. Thus by the end of the decade the number of incidents, the degree of losses and the percentage of total crimes associated with retail premises involving robberies as well as the number of physical injuries sustained by retail staff all declined significantly from the level recorded in the early 1990s. However, the degree of support given to retail staff who have been the victims of robbery has showed no noticeable signs of improvement, and the emphasis remains on training and the development of crime prevention measures rather than on providing increased support and compensation for the victims.

The summary of the findings from the 1994 *Commercial Victimisation Survey* presents a slightly different picture of crimes against retail and manufacturing premises. It found that 4 per cent of premises surveyed had been robbed, while 2 per cent reported incidents of assault in which staff were injured (Mirrlees-Black and Ross 1995). Only 0.7 per cent of premises experienced a robbery involving a firearm, while 1 per cent had been robbed by an offender with a knife. Fifteen per cent of the robberies resulted in injury to staff. The amounts reported stolen varied considerably between different types of premises, with the larger premises experiencing average losses in the region of £2,000 while smaller establishments reported average losses of around £740. Nearly half the retailers surveyed said nothing was stolen in the last robbery they had experienced.

In a more focused study carried out in the Belgrave and West End areas of Leicester in 1995, it was found that 1.8 per cent of manufacturing, 4.0 per cent of wholesale, 4.2 per cent of retailing and 3.4 per cent of the service sector experienced a robbery (Wood *et al* 1996). However, victimisation was not found to be evenly spread across the population but rather concentrated in certain sectors, with some 15 per cent of businesses (135) experiencing 58 per cent of all incidents. It was also found that many small businesses are repeatedly the victims of crime, with the average business experiencing 3.5 incidents of crime each year. The growing recognition of the concentration and compounding of victimisation has led to an increased focus on repeat incidents.

Repeat victimisation

Within the growing body of research on victimisation it has been shown that victimisation is not evenly distributed but tends to be concentrated both socially and geographically. It has been well documented that repeated victimisations occur within a relatively short period of time, and this element of predictability is held to have important implications for crime reduction programmes (Farrell and Pease 1993). It has also been shown that one of the best predictors of whether a certain premises is likely to be victimised is whether it has been victimised in the recent past. Thus, as the *Retail Crime Survey* (1999) and the *Commercial Victimisation Survey* found, a third of the retail premises that had been victimised in 1993 had been victimised ten or more times in that year (Mirrlees-Black and Ross 1995).[2] In a similar vein, Gabor *et al* (1987) noted that about one in five of the premises included in their study were held up seven or more times. Repeat victimisation was found to be particularly concentrated in convenience stores. In all, three out of four of the targets were found to be victims of more than one armed robbery.

An examination of the recorded robberies that occurred in banks and building societies in and around London between 1992 and 1994 reveals that certain banks and branches were disproportionately targets of robberies, with the average branch suffering 1.54 robberies and the most robbed suffering six robberies over the three-year period. Interestingly, repeat robberies tend to be less successful than the first robberies, probably as a consequence of the changes in the security features of each bank or because of greater staff awareness (Matthews *et al* 2001).

Data provided by the Flying Squad (which includes information on every bank and building society robbed in the London area between 1992 and 1994) provided the raw data on which the analysis of repeats was based. In total there were 784 bank robberies and 613 building society robberies (including attempts) distributed among 568 bank and 374 building society branches. Table 5.1 shows the number of victimisations per victimised bank and building society. This table also shows that some 41 per cent of building society branches and some 35 per cent of victimised bank branches experienced more than one robbery. Generally, around 50 per cent of robbed premises will be robbed more than once over a three-year period. Branches that were not robbed more than once in this period included a higher percentages of cases in which the initial robbery was unsuccessful. In the literature on repeat victimisation, repeats tend to occur relatively quickly after the initial incident. In our sample this pattern of repeats was found to occur for both the banks and the building societies (see Figure 5.1).

Table 5.1: Number of victimisations suffered by robbed branches

Robberies	Bank branches	Building society branches
1	327	219
2	115	92
3	45	46
4	14	13
5	6	4
6	1	1

In building societies, nearly one third of all the repeat offences that took place in the two-year period following the initial robbery occurred within two months. The critical question that arises is whether it was the same robbers returning to the scene of the original robbery or whether different robbers were attacking the same premises. The answer to this question would indicate whether repeats are mainly a function of the motivation and experiences of particular robbers or whether they are a function of the characteristics (size, location, design, security etc.) of the premises themselves which make them a more attractive target.

It was evident in the interviews carried out with armed robbers that

Figure 5.1: Time course of repeat victimisations – banks and bulding societies (1992–94)

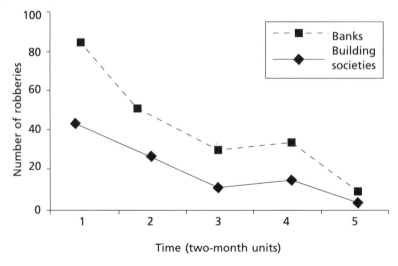

some admitted returning to premises they had previously robbed. The rationales given for returning were either that they knew the layout or that they knew what to expect, and this increased their confidence. In one case a robber returned to a building society branch the next day because he felt he had not been given enough money and came back, as he put it, 'to get the rest'.

Conclusion

The process of robbery victimisation remains under-researched, particularly in relation to the psychological impact and the effectiveness of the various types of protection and support available to employees. The available research suggests that even amongst the larger financial institutions the levels of support provided are variable and, in some organisations and businesses, are minimal. The experience of robbery can and does have a devastating impact upon the lives of its victims although they are often encouraged to play down the effects and to get back to work.

There is little evidence that the guidelines presented by the HSE (1993) have changed practices in banks, building societies or other commercial establishments. The fact there have been no cases brought against employers by the HSE in relation to the legal requirements to protect the health and safety of their employees is indicative of the significance this traumatic form of victimisation has in commercial and official circles. Given the growing body of research carried out in recent years on the impact of other forms of violent crime (such as domestic violence, rape and racial attacks), violence at work in general, and armed robbery in particular, is a conspicuously neglected area.

Much of the available official literature has been concerned with providing guidelines and recommendations rather than detailing obligations and legal requirements. There is little or no discussion on the mechanisms for the enforcement of these requirements or on the penalties for failing to provide adequate protection. Unsurprisingly, the levels of compensation for the victims of robbery tend to be modest and, in the few cases of compensation that arose in the research, the sum payable was reported to be in the region of £1,000.

The largely managerialist approach presented by organisations such as the HSE has been influential. Its recommendations were summarised by the Banking Insurance and Finance Union (1994) and distributed amongst its members.[3] Within this literature, however, there is an assumed consensus over objectives and an implicit belief that employers generally have the best interest of their staff in mind and only need guidance on providing the right kind of security, education and training programmes to maximise their contribution. As we have noted, however, much of the expenditure on security is designed primarily to secure the premises rather than to protect staff. At the same time there may be a conflict of interest between the employer's desire to maximise profits and reduce costs and the objective of providing support and protection for employees. One example of such a conflict of interest is the desire by a number of financial institutions to move towards open-plan 'user-friendly' layouts in their branches in an attempt to attract customers. Such a strategy, however, is likely to make staff more vulnerable to violent attacks. The recent decreases in the number of commercial robberies has been used to justify reductions in the level of support and protection offered to staff. However, those who remain victims will not derive much comfort from these statistical movements and are unlikely to find the experience of robbery any less traumatic.

Among the small businesses that remain the targets of armed robbery, the levels of security, training and support are often minimal. This raises serious problems about the protection of staff. There is growing evidence that the robberies carried out in these premises are likely to be more unpredictable and the perpetrators more desperate and volatile, while the owners may be more reluctant to comply with the robbers' demands. This combination of factors creates a situation in which both physical and psychological victimisation may well increase, even if the total number of commercial robberies continues to go down.

Notes

1 There is, of course, an overlap between racial attacks and robberies and theft from Asian-run shops, as Hibberd and Shapland (1993) have indicated (see also Ekblom and Simon 1988).

2 The *Commercial Victimisation Survey* found that 59 per cent of the full crime count was against 3 per cent of retailing premises (Mirrlees-Black and Ross 1995).

3 The Banking Insurance and Finance Union (BIFU) represented members who worked in banks and building societies. Recently it has amalgamated with other small unions to form the UNIFI, which now represents these employees. However, neither the BIFU nor the UNIFI have carried out any systematic research on behalf of their members to examine the impact of robbery victimisation.

Chapter 6

Policing armed robbery

Introduction

A critical element in the process of solving crimes is the nature of the victim–offender relation. The proximity and intensity of this relation will directly affect the likelihood of an offender being identified and caught. Consequently, the relatively quick and anonymous nature of armed robbery makes it amongst the most difficult crimes to solve. It is for this reason there has been considerable international discussion on the most effective ways to deal with armed robbery and, in particular, on the desirability of establishing dedicated robbery squads that are able to concentrate exclusively on this type of crime.

It has also been the case in recent years that the reliance on traditional methods of detection that involve gathering and piecing together evidence after the event has been called into question. In an influential report published by the Audit Commission entitled *Helping with Enquiries* (1993), the issue of police effectiveness and, particularly, the value of existing forms of investigation have been the object of critical examination. The Audit Commission have strongly suggested that the emphasis should increasingly be on a proactive rather than a reactive approach and should target criminals rather than responding to the reported incidents of crime:

> A consequence of rising workload, some duplication of effort and the paperwork burden is that the focus on detectives' work is upon the crime incident rather than the criminal. This draws them away from the proactive work needed to apprehended those prolific criminals who generate much of the police workload and impose such damage upon communities. A change of emphasis away from

reaction to crime incidents towards strategies for crime reduction and targeting of prolific offenders is needed, although without sacrificing attention to the victims of crime. Proactive work is driven by intelligence information, but in many forces the intelligence function is inadequately equipped with technology and under-staffed. Informants, a highly cost-effective source of detection, are under-used. (Audit Commission 1993: 2)

In advocating greater emphasis on proactive, intelligence-led policing, the Audit Commission have stimulated a debate over the best way to achieve detections, not only in relation to robbery but also in relation to a range of other crimes. This theme has been actively taken up by the Police Research Group in the Home office, who funded a series of studies (including our own work on armed robbery) that aimed to investigate the processes employed by different police forces around the country to detect different types of crime (Stockdale and Gresham 1995; Matthews 1998).

Thus the issue of policing such crimes as armed robbery has become centred around two main themes. The first is the relation between proactive and reactive policing and the second is the advantages and disadvantages of dedicated units. These debates constitute part of a wider ongoing discussion about the appropriate forms of police organisation and the possibility of increasing police effectiveness and accountability, as well as the role of the public police in dealing with different forms of crime (Eck 1983; Bayley 1994).

Dedicated versus non-dedicated units

There are, in essence, four justifications for establishing dedicated or specialist squads for dealing with crime. The first is that the crime concerned is of a serious nature and requires levels of experience and expertise not available within existing police departments. The second is that dedicated units are able to operate more proactively and are able to penetrate criminal networks in ways non-dedicated units may find difficult to do. Thirdly, dedicated units can have a degree of mobility and flexibility that allows them to move beyond conventional policing boundaries. Finally, these units are able to mobilise evidence and gain convictions in cases that may otherwise be difficult to resolve. Whether it be a vice squad, fraud squad, burglary squad or robbery squad, these rationales have historically been used to justify the creation of relatively autonomous units – thus producing a division of labour between different sections of the public police force.

Our own research was set up to review the operation of what is undoubtedly the best known robbery squad in the UK – the Flying Squad based at New Scotland Yard in London – and to compare its approach to a criminal intelligence department (CID) based in South Yorkshire. Originally set up in 1918, the Flying Squad was established as a mobile patrol of 12 detectives who were charged with apprehending criminal gangs, pickpockets, known criminals, 'smash and grab' raiders and bank robbers. A few high-profile arrests in the 1920s (as well as the growing concern about serious crime in London) secured the position of the Flying Squad as a specialist crime-fighting unit (Darbyshire and Hilliard 1993). Since that time the fortunes of the squad have changed dramatically from being seen as the country's elite detective force to an object of derision and of recurring charges of corruption at different times. In the postwar period the remit of the Flying Squad has narrowed from the investigation of most forms of serious crime occurring in the capital to the investigation of serious armed robbery against banks, building societies, post offices, security vans, jewellers and betting shops. Since it was estimated in the 1980s that some 60 per cent of serious armed robberies in England and Wales occur in the London area, the need for such a squad was reaffirmed. However, in recent years charges of corruption and malpractice have resurfaced, and this has raised the question again of whether such a dedicated robbery unit should be maintained (Campbell 1998; Hopkins 2000).

In order to examine the possible advantages of a dedicated unit, research was carried out between 1994 and 1996 that looked at the methods used by the Flying Squad to detect robberies in the London area, and this approach was compared to the CID in South Yorkshire, which dealt with all forms of robbery as well as a range of other serious crimes.

Robbery comprises approximately 10 per cent of the workload of the CID nationally. In most forces armed robbery will be dealt with by the CID, although the Audit Commission (1993) found that detective constables 'may receive little or no guidance or direction about the nature and extent of enquiries to pursue, nor an indication of duration'. The Audit Commission (ibid.) criticised CIDs in general for a lack of effective supervision, for too heavy a workload, for an absence of management information systems and for limited recognition of good detective skills amongst officers. In general the approach of the CID is criticised for being highly reactive and for focusing its efforts on the crime rather than the criminal. Thus the debate about the relative effectiveness of dedicated and non-dedicated units for dealing with armed robbery overlaps with the discussion about the relative merits of proactive versus reactive styles of policing.

Proactive versus reactive policing

The Audit Commission (1990, 1993) noted that some 75 per cent of the work carried out by the CID is reactive and, it claimed this reflects the traditional policing approach that involves responding to individual incidents. On the assumption that a small number of prolific criminals are responsible for a disproportionately large percentage of recorded crime, the Audit Commission in conjunction with the Home Office Police Research Group have called for a greater emphasis on information-led strategies that target prolific criminals. This approach, they argue, would constitute a more effective way of reducing crime.

Thus proactive strategies are seen to be based on gathering information, on a focus on the criminal rather than the crime, on the surveillance of suspects, on developing forms of crime prevention and crime 'watch' schemes and, in particular, on a greater use of informants, who are seen to be extremely cost-effective in assisting with the detection of such crimes as robbery.

Amongst the reactive policing strategies are the various methods of detecting crimes by gathering and piecing together information as a result of an incident being reported to the police. This can involve the use of video images or eye-witness descriptions, the interrogation and interviewing of witnesses and suspects and checking the movements of suspects, collecting forensic evidence, as well as pursuing different forms of detective work that involve looking for leads and attempting to solve cases through the examination and assessment of the available evidence (Eck 1983).

However, as became clear in the course of our research on armed robbery, the distinction between proactive and reactive policing is far from clear cut. This is partly because information comes in a number of different forms and can come into play at different points in the process of investigation. It is, in fact, central to both the identification of offenders and to the detection of reported crimes. In a number of cases information gathered by the police in the process of investigation led to the identification of other suspects, who then became the object of police attention. By the same token the surveillance of known offenders in some cases resulted not in their arrest but served to provide information on crimes that were under investigation. Interviewing suspects in the course of investigating a reported robbery provided a useful source of information, which either alerted the police to the activities of other robbers or actually assisted in the clear-up of robberies that had previously been committed but remained unsolved.

In those cases described as predominantly 'reactive', the investigation of the case does not normally involve the painstaking sifting of evidence. Typically after a robbery has occurred, the detective will talk to victims, suspects and witnesses and will decide fairly quickly whether there is enough evidence to arrest and prosecute suspects with a reasonable likelihood of conviction. Thus as David Bayley (1994: 26–27) found in his international survey of the detection process:

Contrary to their fictional portrayal, detectives quickly formulate a theory about who committed the crime and then set about collecting the evidence that will support arrest and prosecution. Unlike Sherlock Holmes they do not maintain a disinterested open mind. Detectives know that if perpetrators cannot be identified by people on the scene, police are not likely to find the criminals on their own. Nor is physical evidence especially important in determining whether a case is pursued. Physical evidence is used as a confirmation – to support testimony that identifies suspects. It is seldom used diagnostically, to find suspects. The absence of physical evidence might mean that the case cannot be made; it might also disconfirm the theory. But it hardly ever leads to the identification of persons not already suspected by the police...in short, criminal investigators begin with an identification, then collect the evidence; they rarely collect the evidence and then make an identification.

Thus, as Bayley (ibid.) suggests, very little detective work is purely reactive in the sense that it attempts to piece together in a disinterested way the available evidence but, rather, calls on prior knowledge and information to decide whether the case is worth pursuing. This decision will, of course, also be affected by the seriousness of the case, the amount stolen and its public profile.

A central focus of the discussion about the relation between proactive and reactive policing has been the role of informers. Although the use of informers and 'supergrasses' has historically been met with controversy, their use (particularly in the 1970s and 1980s) was positively associated not only with armed robbery but also with drug control, as well as with helping to secure the convictions of a number of high-profile offenders.[1] These convictions suggested that informers could be used effectively to bring serious known criminals to court in cases in which they would otherwise remain immune from prosecution.

The use of informers

The controversy over the use of informers peaked during the 1970s in the UK. A considerable amount of attention was focused at this time on the prolific bank robber, Bertie Smalls, who became the first of a number of 'supergrasses'.[2] He provided incriminating evidence on a number of his associates in exchange for a substantial reduction in his sentence, as well as a share of the insurance rewards. Following the arrests (which resulted from Bertie Smalls' testimony) it was claimed that the number of serious armed robberies decreased by as much as 60 per cent. In the USA the use of informers such as Joe Velachy against organised crime drew public attention to the role informers could play in mobilising evidence against powerful and organised criminals (Albanese 1989; Short 1992; Morton 1995; Greer 2001).

Such information, however, comes at a price. The controversy that surrounded these high-profile cases centred around the injustices that may result from informers being protected by the police or having their sentences significantly reduced. Thus, although the use of informants has in some cases been associated with timely interventions and with the detection and arrest of armed robbers who would otherwise probably not have been caught, their use has also been associated with corruption, dubious methods of recruitment and tasking, inadequate accountability and a lack of proper supervision (Dunningham and Norris 1999; Clarke 2001; South 2001; Williamson and Bagshaw 2001). Critics of the informant system claim that paying known criminals and giving them protection and a degree of immunity can all too easily become a strategy for supporting criminal activity. In some cases informers have been accused of setting up robberies in order to claim a reward or of diverting police attention from their own nefarious activities. Although efforts have been made to tighten controls on the use of informers in recent years through the use of co-handlers as well as through the introduction of a more formalised working relationship, many of the problems of corruption and 'dirty dealing' persist (Hanvey 1995). As Peter Reuter (1983) has argued, there is a reluctance both on the part of the police and the informant to formalise the relationship, and attempts to do so will lead either to the loss of informants or to the evasion of guidelines. If there are too many constraints, the informant system (which itself is inherently unstable and often short term) may break down. Thus Reuter (ibid.) concludes: ' ... either we must accept the tensions created by ill-monitored licensing, or we must lower the demands on the police to apprehend certain classes of villains.'

It is for these reasons, coupled with concerns about the quality of the information provided by some informants, that there is considerable reluctance amongst certain detectives to use informers. Some police officers also feel uncomfortable about collaborating with the 'enemy' in their attempts to win the 'war against crime'. Mike Maguire and Timothy John (1995) found in their survey of informers that only half the CID officers they questioned had paid informants and, of these, the majority had only one or two. They found, however, that some police departments had 'casual informers' who did not want a formalised relationship with the police. There were also found to be some reservations about the quality and reliability of the information provided by informers. It soon becomes apparent to detectives that quality information is normally only available from the more accomplished criminals. As one police officer put it: 'If you want good information on serious villains you don't ask Mother Teresa.' However, the type of offenders who are likely to have useful information are precisely those who are seen as 'trouble' by police officers, while hardened criminals are likely, over a period of time, to have built up a considerable resentment and hostility to the police.

There are issues about how much, if anything, informers should be paid. It is evident that the pool of money available in most forces is not great, and our research found that Flying Squad officers, who tended to be particularly active in running informers, had a total annual budget of £120,000. On top of this, rewards are also paid by insurance companies and commercial institutions for information leading to arrest. From the available figures it appears that each of the 100 registered informants was paid about £1,000 each on average each year.

Apart from registered and casual informers there are those who turn informer once caught and who provide information on either their accomplices or on other criminals in order to reduce their sentence. Finally, there are what we might call 'citizen' informers who provide information on suspicious persons or who have information on specific offenders. These may be spontaneous contacts or they may be prompted by programmes such as *Crimewatch*. Thus informers can be divided into those who come into direct contact with the police (who will normally themselves be offenders) and 'active citizens'. Alternatively, informers may be divided between those who are long term and those who provide information on a specific case. When making claims about the use of informers it is important to bear these distinctions in mind and to determine, as far as possible, which type of informer is the most useful.

The use of informers has been limited by the rules of disclosure and the problems the police have in protecting their informers from identification in court. If the identification of informants is asked for by the court, the police will normally drop the case rather than reveal the identity of their sources. According to the Flying Squad officers who were interviewed, around 50 cases are 'lost' on this basis every year. Whether or not these lost cases are taken into account when evaluating the use of informers depends upon the type of measures being used to assess different proactive or reactive approaches. In a climate in which police activities are increasingly evaluated in terms of cost-effectiveness, it is necessary to clarify, as far as possible, how effectiveness is to be measured.

Measuring effectiveness

One of the most frequently asked questions nowadays in relation to policing and other criminal justice activities is 'what works?' Assessing what works in relation to policing is bound up with the types of measures used. One of the measures most frequently used by the police and evaluators is the clear-up rate. However, the meaning of 'clear-up' is far from clear. The standard conception of the clear-up rate is the proportion of offences recorded by the police that are 'detected' each year. For most crimes this 'rate' or, rather, the proportion of known offences detected, has been falling steadily over the past two decades.

If the 'clear-up' rate is, however, to be used as a gauge of effectiveness, some consideration needs to be given to the number of incidents recorded, their seriousness and the number of officers employed over time. Thus it may be that the number of crimes cleared up per officer may increase at a time when the overall clear-up rate is declining. However, the main difficulty in using clear-up rates as a measure of effectiveness is that the term 'clear-up' can cover a number of processes, including: 1) if a person has been charged, summonsed or cautioned for the offence; 2) if the offence has been admitted and has been or could be taken into consideration by the court; and 3) if there is sufficient evidence to charge a person but the case is not proceeded with (Bottomley and Coleman 1995). Thus crimes can in fact be 'cleared up' without any direct police 'detection' work being undertaken, and there is a well established and important distinction between 'primary' clear-ups resulting from direct police detection work and 'secondary' clear-ups in which offenders may be persuaded to have other offences 'taken into consideration' by the court (Walker 1992).

For these reasons comparisons between the clear-up rates of the different forces are very problematic. The context, type of offenders, seriousness of the crimes and the like will all independently affect the clear-up rate irrespective of police activity. For these reasons arrest rates and conviction rates have been used instead as measures of police performance.

Whether we use the clear-up rate, arrests or convictions as a measure of police effectiveness, there remains an unresolved tension between placing greater emphasis on proactive policing and simultaneously arguing for greater police effectiveness in terms of the standard measures. The focus on the more serious criminals is likely to decrease the proportion of crimes cleared up, as well as the number of arrests and convictions. It is, paradoxically, precisely because the police are placed under pressure from organisations like the Audit Commission and the Home Office to reach performance 'targets' and improve clear-ups that they gravitate towards those recorded crimes that are most easily detectable and maintain the emphasis on 'reactive' strategies. Targeting serious and prolific criminals, placing them under surveillance and gathering information can be an extremely time-consuming activity whose outcome is uncertain. It is often easier to achieve results by 'rounding up the usual suspects' once a robbery has been committed (Gill 2000).

The research

Having taken some account of the methodological and conceptual difficulties of assessing the effectiveness of different approaches to the policing of crimes such as armed robbery, our research aimed to uncover the strategies by which commercial robberies were detected through an examination of a sample of cases in London and all the recorded armed robberies in South Yorkshire for 1993. The London sample involved 235 cases out of a total of 1,193 recorded Band 1 robberies. The number of recorded armed robberies in South Yorkshire for that year was 165. Figures 6.1 and 6.2 show the distribution of armed robberies in the two locations between different targets.

It is evident that the distribution of armed robberies in the London area is significantly greater than that of South Yorkshire, with over 40 times as many bank robberies and 25 times as many building society robberies. In South Yorkshire Band 2 robberies – shops, garages, licensed premises and the like – accounted for approximately half the armed robberies with which the CID had to deal. Significantly, almost one third of the total of 165 recorded armed robberies in 1993 were 'unsuccessful'.

It also became apparent in the course of the research that the profile of armed robbers was distinctly different in the two areas. Although just over half of those arrested for armed robbery in South Yorkshire in 1993 had previous convictions for either burglary or robbery, the choice of

Figure 6.1: Number of Band 1 and Band 2 armed robberies in the MPD (1987–94).

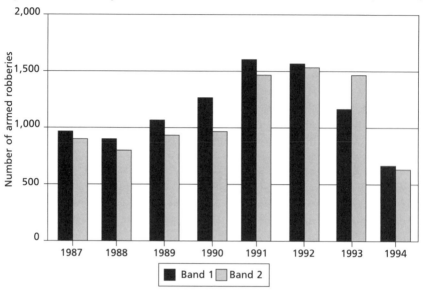

Figure 6.2: Number of Band 1 and Band 2 armed robberies in South Yorkshire (1987–94).

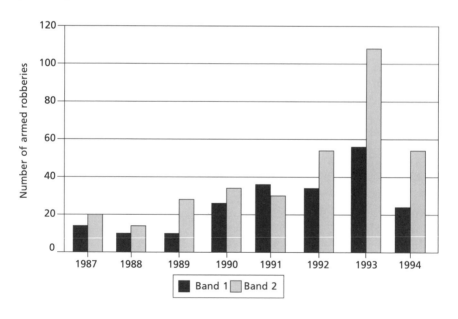

targets and the high percentage of unsuccessful cases indicate that a high proportion of those carrying out commercial robberies were amateurs or intermediates rather than professionals. Although the profile of known armed robbers in the London area also included a significant percentage of amateurs and intermediates, it was apparent there was also a substantial number of professional robbers who organised relatively well planned raids against security vehicles and jewellers as well as banks and building societies.

There were also important geographical differences between the two areas studied. The Metropolitan area is, of course, a sprawling urban mix of residential, industrial and commercial activity with a population in excess of 10 million. South Yorkshire, in contrast, incorporates a small number of urban centres – principally Sheffield, Rotherham and Barnsley – as well as surrounding suburban and rural areas that cover an area of 600 square miles with a population of around 1,300,000. Nearly two thirds of the county's armed robberies were committed in Sheffield in 1993, with Doncaster accounting for 15 per cent, Barnsley 12 per cent and Rotherham 17 per cent (Talbot 1994).

At the time the research was carried out, both forces were going through a period of review and reorganisation. This had both a positive and negative impact on the research. On the positive side it raised a number of issues in the officers' minds about the appropriate organisational arrangements to deal with armed robbery. On the negative side restructuring brought an element of uncertainty into the situation and made some officers reluctant to be frank and open lest critical comments might feed into the reassessment exercise, resulting in negative consequences.

In the period preceeding the research, both forces had been experiencing a steady increase in the number of armed robberies in their respective areas. In the Metropolitan region the number of Band 1 robberies recorded between 1987 and 1993 had increased from under 1,000 to approximately 1,100, having peaked at 1,600 in 1991. In South Yorkshire over the same period the number of Band 1 robberies had increased from 15 to 58, while the number of Band 2 robberies had increased alarmingly from 20 to over 100.

Both forces, however, were claiming impressively high clear-up rates for armed robbery, with South Yorkshire clearing up 30 per cent of all recorded armed robberies and almost 50 per cent of building society robberies. The Flying Squad were recording a similar clear-up rate for commercial robberies in general and a 60 per cent clear-up rate for banks. The aim of the research was to investigate the process by which commercial robberies were detected in both areas. Particular attention was paid to the differences between the mainly proactive approach adopted by the dedicated unit – the Flying Squad – as well as to the reactive and non-dedicated nature of the South Yorkshire CID. Working primarily from the 1993 police reports in both areas the research aimed to assess the effectiveness of the different methods of detection employed.

Detecting armed robberies

Determining the principal reason for detection and arrest is a difficult operation. In each of the cases examined, interviews were conducted with the arresting officer and the documentation relating to each case was analysed. In the majority of cases there were a number of overlapping factors that made an arrest possible. However, a comparison between the processes of detection in London and South Yorkshire revealed a very different distribution of the principal reasons for detecting commercial robberies. There was also a noticeable difference in the clear-up rate for armed robbery for different commercial targets in the two locations. As Table 6.1 indicates, the clear-up rate for banks and building societies is considerably higher than that for post offices, off-licences, garages and shops.

Table 6.1: Detection rate of armed robberies by target (1993).

| | MPD | | South Yorkshire | |
Premises	Total no.	Clear-up rate (%)	Total no.	Clear-up rate (%)
Bank	159	60	11	36
Building society	111	53	21	47
Post office	26	18	21	33
Cash-in-transit	6	12	–	–
Betting shop	56	14	6	75
Jewellers	17	27	–	–
Licensed premises	–	–	11	45
Shop	–	–	26	23
Garage	–	–	18	27

Although these detection rates in both locations show a fairly consistent relation between softer targets and lower clear-up rates it is the case (particularly in South Yorkshire) that because of the small number of cases involved in certain categories it is possible easily to distort the profile. In relation to betting-shop robberies in South Yorkshire, for example, there was only a total of six cases and four were cleared up, giving a percentage detection rate that is considerably higher than would have been expected in a larger sample. It is clear that the type of target, its level of vulnerability and the type of robber it attracts have an effect on the clear-up rate that is relatively independent of police strategy. However, what remains unclear is the relative impact of these three factors.

As Table 6.2 indicates, there were significant differences between the two locations in how detection or arrest came about. In London the role of informers was central to the process of detection, while in South Yorkshire, informers played a lesser role with rapid police response accounting for almost a quarter of arrests. A third of the detections came from clear-ups arising from information gathered while offenders were in police custody.

Table 6.2:. Principal reasons for arrest and/or detection in Metropolitan Police Department and South Yorkshire (1993).

| | MPD | | South Yorkshire | |
	No.	%	No.	%
Caught at or near scene				
Public initiated	9	8	1	2
Police initiated	14	13	11	23
Subsequent police investigations				
Video/photo	6	6	4	9
Informant	43	40	8	17
Forensic	7	7	1	2
Surveillance	4	4	4	9
Admitted while in custody	4	4	17	36
Protracted police inquiries (3 months or over)	21	19	1	2
Total	108	100	47	100

Caught at or near the scene

In London and South Yorkshire it was found that just over 20 per cent of cases involved the offender being caught at or near the scene of the crime. These cases can be divided into those that were public initiated and those that were police initiated. Public-initiated arrests were the result either of staff 'having a go' or raising the alarm while containing the robbers. In a few cases the arrest resulted directly from the identification of suspects by staff or witnesses.

Police-initiated investigations at or near the scene were the primary reason for some 13 per cent of arrests in London and 23 per cent in South Yorkshire. However, in both locations the processes underlying the arrests were very different. In London they mainly arose from police intelligence gleaned from informers and surveillance operations, while in South Yorkshire they resulted from a rapid armed police response to information gathered at the scene from witnesses and victims. The layout of the road system (particularly in Sheffield) allowed the South Yorkshire police to respond quickly in vehicles by blocking the roads out of the city and by securing arrests in the areas where robberies were reported. In 10 of the 11 cases arising in South Yorkshire that were police initiated, the offenders were caught within a four-mile radius of the scene of the crime. In these cases the police either acted upon descriptions of suspects provided by members of the public or they stopped vehicles matching the car descriptions or registration numbers reported to the police. In both locations there were also a limited number of arrests that resulted from chance occurrences whereby uniformed police spotted suspicious circumstances and acted immediately. A small number of arrests occurred as a result of stop-and-search operations.

How do the police hear about incidents? Research by Bernard Rix and colleagues, which was based on an examination of 5,000 firearms incidents on the Force's Command and Dispatch system, found that:

Not surprisingly, police are most likely to hear about firearms incidents through 999 calls (43%), although other non-emergency phone calls are also a significant method of informing police of incidents (32%). The use of the 999 operator is particularly high amongst commercial premises (bookmakers 88%; off-licence 84%; newsagents 72%) compared to residential premises (39%). Auto-alarms are a significant source only where banks and building societies are involved (22%), although this method of raising the alarm was also used by 8% of cash-in-transit targets. Officers on patrol rarely reported incidents, only in 8% of cash in transit robberies and 4% of incidents involving banks and building societies and residential premises. Overall, pre-planned police operations accounted for 7% of reports, targeted at 10% of incidents involving residential premises and 9% of sub-post offices and banks and building societies. (Rix *et al* 1998: 10–11)

Subsequent police investigations

Those robberies that were not cleared up immediately or shortly after the incident were detected as a result of a number of different processes. These included video and photographic evidence, the use of informants and forensic or surveillance operations in which suspects were monitored.

Video and photographic evidence
Despite the growing emphasis that has been placed upon the use of video equipment in commercial premises, the percentage of arrests in which video evidence played a primary role was much less than expected in both locations. Improvements in the quality of video images, as well as the introduction of 35 mm lens cameras, have undoubtedly increased the chances of arrest and conviction in a number of cases. However, of the 108 cases in which arrests were made in the London area, only 52 had usable video evidence. Of these images, three were described as 'excellent', four as 'good', three as 'fair' and six as 'poor'. In a further four cases cameras were present but either had no film or were not activated. In South Yorkshire video evidence was available only in about one third of cases. Of these, video evidence did or could have assisted in identifying the offender in some way, although in five instances they were of use only in identifying clothing, hats or jewellery rather than facial features. Video evidence was the principal reason for arrest in four cases in South Yorkshire. The main role of video evidence was to provide supporting and corroborative evidence and, in some cases, it was influential either in prompting admissions or in enabling detectives to link different incidents. It should also be noted that even in cases in which good video evidence was available it was not always possible to trace the offender.

Informers
The use of and attitude towards informers were considerably different in London and in South Yorkshire. Whereas the Flying Squad officers were selected, in part, on the basis of their ability to cultivate and run informers, the CID officers in South Yorkshire expressed a disdain for informers and were in many cases reticent to use them, particularly known criminals. The differential use of informers in the two forces was also influenced by the type of offender with which the respective forces were concerned. Informers were used in both proactive and reactive ways and some 40 per cent of the robberies cleared up in the London area were the result of information provided by informers after the robbery had occurred. However, while it was the case that paid and registered

informers were instrumental in providing information that allowed the police to make arrests at or near the scene of the robbery, those robberies that were cleared up as a result of robberies being reported and investigated involved not only paid and registered informers but also offenders who provided information on their co-accused (as well as members of the public volunteering information about specific offenders). When the quality of information provided was good, the system of informers appeared to be an extremely useful strategy in detecting robberies. As one senior officer put it: 'One phone call from an informant can be worth a month's detective work.'

Forensic evidence

The availability of good forensic evidence was critical in 7 per cent of the arrests made by the Flying Squad but in only 2 per cent of cases in South Yorkshire. However, forensic evidence played a useful corroborative role in a number of cases, and the Flying Squad benefited from having their own forensic team, which was both accessible and reliable. In the main, forensic evidence was useful in identifying offenders through the examination of discarded clothing and through the analysis of the fingerprints found on the retrieved weapons or recovered vehicles.

Surveillance

Surveillance, like the use of informers, played both a proactive and reactive role. It was used proactively to keep those suspected of planning robberies under observation and reactively to monitor the movements and activities of those suspected of having committed a crime. While only 4 per cent of robberies in the Metropolitan area were cleared up primarily as a consequence of the use of surveillance, it proved to be useful in a number of cases in gathering the evidence that eventually led to an arrest. The Flying Squad have their own specialist surveillance unit as well as access to other surveillance teams when required. Surveillance technologies were employed in 36 per cent of the cases examined in the London area and were seen as being important in linking offences and offenders.

Indicatively, in South Yorkshire there were only four robberies that were detected primarily through surveillance operations. In one case an operation was set up to target a number of people suspected of committing a string of post office robberies. This operation, however, was brought to a halt when one of the main suspects shot and wounded one of the others.

Admissions while in police custody

There was a marked difference in the detection of robberies resulting from the direct questioning of suspects by the police and from robbers admitting their involvement in armed robberies while being held on other charges in the two force areas. Surprisingly, the percentage of robberies detected in this way by the Flying Squad was relatively small (4 per cent). In South Yorkshire, on the other hand, 36 per cent of offenders made admissions during interviews while detained at the police station. These admissions were usually made in the face of considerable, if not overwhelming, evidence. The difference in the role of interviewing in making arrests between the two forces may also have been a consequence of the South Yorkshire officers having better access to local information and some knowledge of the 'villains' operating in their area. In addition, where prolific offenders in South Yorkshire were identified and arrested they made a considerable impact on the overall clear-up rate, given the relatively low number of robberies. When arrests are achieved through the direct questioning of suspects, this is a cost-effective method of clearing up crime since it requires few resources and relies mainly on the skills of the investigating officer in exploiting the vulnerability of the suspect. In areas with a large percentage of amateur and inexperienced robbers, such an approach can pay dividends.

Protracted police investigations.

If it is decided particular cases are to be investigated, there is normally an expectation they will be cleared up fairly quickly. However, some cases are deemed to be serious enough to warrant protracted police inquiries. Approximately 20 per cent of cases conducted by the Flying Squad were under investigation for three months or longer. In some cases the investigation was delayed by difficulties in mobilising evidence or in locating the suspects. This was particularly evident in cases where offenders had absconded from prison or had failed to return after home leave. Data supplied by the Flying Squad indicated 17 people were arrested in 1993–94 for carrying out armed robberies while absconding from prison.

In South Yorkshire only one cash was detected as a result of protracted detective work. In such cases attempts are normally made to connect offenders with certain types of robberies by examining different modus operandi and the selection of targets. The importance of linking offences with offenders was made apparent in one of the celebrated cases in South Yorkshire in the early 1990s involving the so-called 'Kagoul robber', who was repeatedly spotted on security cameras wearing distinctive clothing.

He was wanted by six police forces for questioning and had carried out at least 100 robberies in the Midlands and Yorkshire (McLeod 1994).[3] Photographs of the Kagoul robber were displayed publicly and a reward was offered, but police efforts met with little success. The police, however, eventually caught the robber by mapping out his movements between targets and they realised he was travelling by train to each of the robberies. Hence they eventually worked out where he lived.

Research carried out in London by Shona Morrison and Ian O'Donnell (1994) found that, of those robbers who were eventually arrested, 16 per cent were arrested at the scene of the crime (with 70 per cent being police initiated). Twenty-one per cent were arrested later the same day the offence took place and, within four weeks of the robbery, a further 18 per cent were arrested. By six months after the event, another 31 per cent had been caught.

Michael Creedon's (1992) study of the policing of armed robbery in Leicestershire and Northamptonshire found that the key processes of detecting armed robberies were similar in many respects to those of South Yorkshire. In Leicestershire and Northamptonshire a minimal emphasis was placed upon the use of informers, while a greater reliance was placed on interviewing skills in the process of investigation. Gaining admissions while the offender was in police custody accounted for nearly half of the arrests in his sample. This was primarily achieved through police interviewing skills combined with the 'utter ineptitude of some of the offenders'. Again, forensic and video evidence played a mainly corroborated role in the process of detection.

John Conklin's study (1972) of robbery in the USA, which employed a slightly different system of classification, found that 17.5 per cent of robbers were arrested at the scene of the crime, 27 per cent as a result of victim identification, 25 per cent through the identification of a suspect in another case, 10 per cent through multiple confessions and 20 per cent through police investigations. He also noted some significant variation between the clearance of cases involving small and large commercial premises. John Eck (1983, 1992) has shown in his survey of American research on criminal investigation that well trained, well motivated detectives can have a significant impact on the detection and arrest rates for such crimes as robbery. The cultivation of investigative skills, the difficulties of identifying and catching the more professional robbers, could result in policing falling between these two stools, leading to a gradual decline in arrest rates. Eck's data suggest that informers are generally of limited utility in detecting robberies and that informers raise a number of ethical issues as well as questions of accountability. He found that one of the major uses of informants was in relation to the gathering of information in response to the investigation of a reported incident.

Prosecuting and sentencing offenders

Different factors affect the processes of detection and prosecution and those factors that play a primary role in the process of detection may play only a secondary or corroborative role in the prosecution process. Most robbers plead guilty. Only four cases in the London sample pleaded not guilty, although in our sample there were still 44 cases (53 per cent) that were awaiting trial at the time the research was completed. Police officers who were interviewed said they had a good working relationship with the Crown Prosecution Service (CPS), although problems arose in relation to the identification of offenders, the fallibility of witnesses and, in some cases, the reluctance of witnesses to give evidence in court (Maynard 1994).

In South Yorkshire, 44 per cent of convictions were the result of admissions while in a further 27 per cent of cases the main factor was the recovery of property, firearms, clothing or the vehicle. Identification by the victim or witnesses was critical in 18 per cent of cases. In four cases the prosecution was discontinued and in a further two cases the charges of armed robbery were replaced by amended charges. Although a number of the police officers interviewed expressed dismay at the discontinuance of cases by the CPS, the number involved was in fact relatively low. Of the four cases discontinued, one was due to a break in the continuity of evidence and in another the identification evidence was not corroborated in court. In two other cases the police dropped charges against the suspects and discontinued the cases after seeking advice from the CPS.

Although the length of sentence individual robbers were given was influenced by the number of previous convictions and the perceived seriousness of the offence, combined with the actual or potential impact on the victims, there did appear to be a number of serious inconsistencies in the sentencing of armed robbers. In one case in South Yorkshire, for example, two brothers who had robbed a security van were given 12 years each, despite the fact neither had any previous convictions. The judge justified such a long sentence on the grounds that they had abducted a security guard and because one of the offenders had been employed by the company. Despite the generally long sentences given to those convicted of armed robbery, a number of the police officers who were interviewed complained about the 'courts being too lenient'. The available evidence, however, does not support this view. Sentence lengths for robbery in England and Wales, in fact, increased from an average of 38.5 months in 1981 to 47.5 months in 1991. National data indicate that some 75 per cent of those convicted of robbery receive a custodial sentence and that almost 60 per cent of first offenders also receive a custodial sentence (Flood-Paige and Mackie 1998). The introduction of 'three strikes' type legislation in both Britain and the USA means those repeatedly convicted of armed robbery will now serve extremely long sentences.

As noted above (see Chapter 4), inconsistencies in sentencing armed robbers arises mainly from the interpretation of the term 'armed' and from the lack of a clear distinction in court between those carrying real, imitation, loaded or unloaded firearms. The failure of British courts to take into account the ability and the intention of the 'armed' robber to inflict harm on his victims means that, in practice, there is no disincentive for robbers to carry real and loaded firearms. Any rational sentencing policy would provide every incentive for robbers not to carry real and loaded firearms, rather than justifying current sentencing policy in relation to the perceived threat to the victim. In general, greater consideration needs to be given to the intentions of the offender as well as to the potential threat to future victims.

Conclusion

The rapid and impersonal nature of commercial armed robberies makes it a difficult crime to police effectively. For this reason, dedicated units such as the Flying Squad in London have been set up to penetrate criminal networks and to develop a more proactive approach. The arrest and conviction of a number of leading underworld figures and notorious villains in the 1960s and the 1970s established the Flying Squad as an elite crime-fighting unit. The recent foiling of the Dome robbery in London (which involved an attempt to steal, James Bond style, one of the world's most valuable diamonds) underlined the value of good information in preventing a potentially costly, not to say embarrassing, robbery from taking place (Hopkins and Braningen 2000).[4]

Some of the more unsavoury practices that have been associated with members of the Flying Squad in recent years involving corruption and the consequent suspension of six officers have, however, called into question the role of dedicated robbery units (Campbell 1998). These concerns have also been put into a new perspective by the intervention of the influential Audit Commission and, particularly, by its call for the development of more proactive forms of policing, involving the targeting of prolific offenders rather than reacting to criminal incidents. The growing emphasis on proactive policing has been echoed by the Home Office Police Research Group. It is suggested that placing greater emphasis on proactive policing is the most effective way to improve police performance.

However, the evidence for developing more proactive forms of intervention is far from conclusive. There are conceptual and practical difficulties associated with this proposal. The conceptual difficulties centre around seeing proactive and reactive policing as oppositional strategies rather than as overlapping and mutually reinforcing options. This in turn is associated with some confusion between the roles of information, intelligence and informers. All good police work is dependent on the flow of information and reactive policing is no less dependent upon information, and intelligence or the use of informers than proactive strategies.

The police as 'knowledge workers' (Ericson and Haggerty 1997) are involved mainly in the business of gathering and processing information. The main problem confronting police nowadays is not so much the quantity of information but, rather, the quality of information available, and police departments are increasingly faced with a growing problem of information overload. Consequently, the issue is not so much one of gathering information but its analysis, interpretation and verification. For information to be translated into 'intelligence' it needs to be ordered, sifted, cleansed and analysed. Where proactive strategies have been shown to work their effectiveness has often been local and temporary (Chatterton 1987; Stockdale and Gresham 1995). Robert Heaton (2000), however, concluded in his review of proactive policing in the USA that placing a greater emphasis on proactive policing has little discernible effect upon overall crime levels or detection rates.

It may appear at first sight that informers represent an extremely cost-effective way of clearing up such crimes as armed robbery. But when the full cost of recruiting, cultivating, supervising and administering informers is taken into account, their cost-effectiveness is questionable. Nevertheless, the increased pressure to recruit a greater number of informers can, as Colin Dunningham and Clive Norris (1999) have suggested, lead to a decrease in respect for the police since their activities are seen to be governed less by a sense of fairness and justice and more by a simple utilitarian expediency. Moreover, the use of informers can place a strain not only on the police force itself but can also create tensions between the police and other criminal justice agencies (Norris and Dunningham 2000). It also increases the expectation that, if a person is prepared to trade information, the judicial consequences of criminal activity can be avoided. These developments may, in turn, lead to a decline in public confidence in the police and, consequently, to a reduction in public co-operation, which has been shown to be pivotal in the development of effective policing (Kinsey *et al* 1986). Simple calculations of cost-effectiveness can be misleading and should be treated with extreme caution. Whether used proactively or reactively, the information provided by informers is of variable quality. Informers can take a considerable amount of time to cultivate and carry costs as well as benefits.

As Gary Marx (1988) has pointed out, informing in its various guises is popularly seen as an element of good citizenship. The introduction of a number of 'hotlines' designed to facilitate the reporting of offenders to the police and other agencies has, however, been dwarfed by the growth of much more elaborate data banks and electronic surveillance systems that are capable of monitoring our behaviour continuously and observing our transactions (Kinnes 2000).

Informers are only of use proactively if there is an identifiable pool of professional and persistent 'villains' who can be 'netted'. Even when such a pool of persistent armed robbers is available there are ethical, legal and practical difficulties in using registered informers. As we have seen in South Yorkshire and elsewhere, the pool of persistent armed robbers is relatively small and the majority of those carrying out commercial robberies are amateurs and novices who are largely unknown to the police and, therefore, gathering information and developing intelligence are likely to be very difficult and time consuming. In the time it takes to identify these robbers proactively, a number of reported incidents could be investigated and cleared up. Whatever lip service the police pay to placing greater emphasis on proactive policing, in practice the balance between proactive and reactive styles of investigation is not an a priori decision but is dependent on the nature and composition of those offenders in any particular area who are likely to engage in armed robbery. Thus rather than pursuing the kind of 'one size fits all' strategy such as that advocated by the Audit Commission, it would be more useful to develop a differentiated and flexible response that is sensitive to the composition of those engaged in armed robbery and to the context in which these robberies are carried out.

It has been apparent over the last few years that the pool of professional armed robbers in the London area is decreasing. Consequently, the brief of the Flying Squad has changed recently. They are now required to deal with all robberies where a firearm is used or intimated, as well as with all robberies involving security vehicles, banks, building societies, post offices, betting shops, jewellers and casinos, whether the robber was armed or not (see Figure 6.3). The decline in Band 1 robberies since 1993 means the Flying Squad are now dealing with an increasing number of softer targets, such as shops, garages, off-licences and the like and, consequently, with a greater percentage of opportunistic robberies carried out by unknown and inexperienced offenders. At the same time the number of professional career robbers appears to be declining gradually. The net result of these two tendencies is the clear-up rate has steadily decreased from 32 per cent in 1993 to 21.5 per cent in 1999. This is mainly because the Flying Squad have changed their style of investigation. If anything, they are now more computerised and produce more information but changes in the type of offenders carrying out the robberies and the style of the robbery (as well as the choice of target) make these offences much more difficult to solve. It is one of the paradoxes of armed robberies that there is an inverse relationship between the inexperience and spontaneity of offenders and

Figure 6.3: Number of robberies dealt with by the Flying Squad (1991–99)

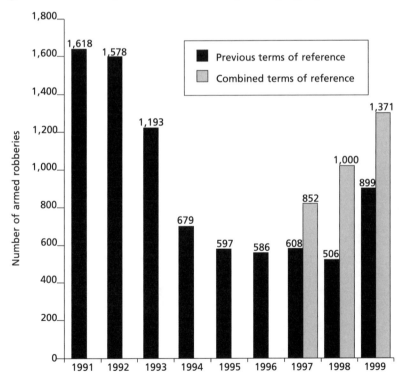

the detection rate. Thus robberies committed against well protected financial institutions that involve some planning tend to be those that are most often solved (Gagnon and LeBlanc 1983).

These developments, in fact, raise the issue of the justification for maintaining a dedicated robbery unit. Interestingly, the only other dedicated robbery unit in operation in the UK during the 1990s was in Nottingham. However, the number of armed robberies in the Nottingham area decreased by over 50 per cent, from 128 to 57 between 1992 and 1994. This level of armed robbery was considered too low to justify a specialist squad, and so the investigation of armed robbery became incorporated into the work of the CID. Although the number of Band 1 armed robberies had decreased in the Metropolitan area from 1,618 in 1991 to 899 in 1999, the wider remit of the Flying Squad meant they were still dealing with a total of 1,371 commercial robberies in 1999 (see Figure 6.3). However, it may be that if the Flying Squad are to continue in operation and to maintain a viable clear-up rate, they may have to rethink their reliance on proactive policing and develop instead a more intensive reactive approach. They may also need to be less elitist and to work more closely with uniformed officers in order to gather information, to develop a faster response and to help identify possible suspects. That is, rather than focus on the internal management structure (as the Audit Commission have suggested) it might be more appropriate to develop more effective systems of communication between Flying Squad officers and those front-line officers who may be in a position to help with inquiries but who at the moment feel marginal and, in some cases, resentful of elite units like the Flying Squad.

By the same token, the Audit Commission's emphasis on targeting 'known' offenders is likely to result in the 'rounding up of the usual suspects' and in depressing rather than improving the clear-up rate (Gill 2000). Although those caught may be the more serious robbers, the probability is that a general shift from responding to reported incidents to the targeting of prolific criminals will decrease the number of robberies cleared up. This raises the central tension in the approach advocated by the Audit Commission, who want the focus to be increasingly on prolific criminals but who, at the same time, are putting the police under pressure to increase clear-up rates. This produces a 'no-win' option that is increasingly likely to create uncertainty and despondency amongst police officers. Creating such tensions is not a recipe for better policing but for encouraging departments to massage clear-up rates by increasing secondary clear-ups and by developing other forms of creative accounting (Young 1991; Davis 1999; Loveday 2000; Jones 2001).

Thus despite all the rhetoric associated with the benefits of proactive policing (particularly the targeting of known criminals), the available evidence suggests this approach is of diminishing utility in respect to recent developments in armed robbery. The apparent decline in the number of known, professional commercial robbers makes a proactive strategy less and less tenable, while the changes in the nature of the targets selected means policing strategies will have to be adjusted in order to come to terms with this changing situation.

Notes

1 Complaints about the use of informers increased during the 1990s in the UK. A number of stories at this time focused on corruption and particularly on how police informers set up crimes in order to turn informer and receive police funds while carrying out their own illicit activities. In one bizarre case an informant sued the Metropolitan Police because he claimed the police had not paid him the money they had promised him for providing information on a number of drug dealers (Perry 2000).

2 Bertie Smalls was a well-known bank robber in the 1970s, and he was arrested for a robbery that involved about £1 million. It was anticipated he would receive a sentence in the region of 15 years but he offered the names of his accomplices in exchange for his freedom. On the basis of the evidence he offered, 25 people were arrested. When his case came to court in July 1973, no evidence was offered against him (Seymour 1982).

3 The so-called 'Kagoul robber' carried out over 100 raids and netted about £100,000. In 1994 he was wanted by six different police forces in the Midlands and South Yorkshire. The interesting thing about him was that he was videoed on many occasions: full facial photographs were available and he was featured on *Crimewatch*. Despite this exposure he was not caught through police identification or through information provided by the public (McLeod 1994).

4 The Dome robbery involved the planned theft of the 203-carat Millennium Star diamond. The Millennium Star is one of the most valuable stones ever cut, with an estimated value of £350 million. The robbery was foiled by the Flying Squad as a result of a tip-off from an informer.

Chapter 7

The demise of armed robbery?

Introduction

Whereas the 1970s and 1980s witnessed a steady increased in armed robbery against commercial targets in England and Wales, there has been a dramatic downturn in the number of recorded commercial robberies since the early 1990s. What is significant about this decrease is that it involves nearly all commercial targets to different degrees. As Table 7.1 indicates, the number of robberies in which firearms were reported to have been used peaked in 1993 and thereafter decreased by 50 per cent by 1998–99. The most significant decreases have occurred in relation to banks and building societies, while reductions in the number of robberies against shops, garages and post offices have been slightly less.

Although the data presented in this table are remarkable, the table does not provide any indication of possible regional variations. Statistics generated by the Flying Squad, however, both confirm and extend the picture presented in the official national criminal statistics. In the London area, Band 1 commercial robberies peaked in 1991 at just over 1,600 and, by 1998 they had fallen to 566, increasing the following year to just under 900. As Figure 7.1 indicates, there has been a considerable decrease in recorded armed robberies against commercial premises in general, despite a surprising, if short-lived, increase in betting-shop robberies and robberies from jewellers shops in 1998–99. In line with the national trend, banks and building societies have decreased significantly.

Interestingly, there has been a decrease in the number of recorded robberies in the USA over a similar period, as well as in other serious violent crimes such as homicide (Blumstein and Wallman 2000). In both Britain and the USA serious violent crime (as well as property crime) has levelled out or decreased over the last decade much to the surprise of

Table 7.1: Number of robberies recorded by the police in England and Wales in which firearms were reported to have been used (by location of offence).

Year	Total	Shop, stall, etc	Garage, service station	Post office	Bank	Building society	Residential	Public highway	Other premises or open space
1988	2,688	666	244	209	210	385	100	441	433
1989	3,390	858	410	319	236	581	100	378	508
1990	3,939	1,022	508	360	296	720	95	441	497
1991	5,296	1,451	508	362	471	924	127	636	817
1992	5,859	1,632	578	464	584	696	212	773	920
1993	6,012	1,711	452	554	498	607	233	940	1,017
1994	4,239	1,106	292	342	288	336	178	1,001	696
1995	4,206	1,193	331	392	240	281	176	930	663
1996	4,013	1,267	309	385	159	144	178	984	587
1997	3,029	933	208	290	134	111	103	832	418
1997–98	2,939	928	188	276	123	91	119	800	414
1998–99	2,973	998	198	282	129	95	109	741	421

Source: Home Office (2000).

Figure 7.1: Commercial robberies dealt with by the Flying Squad (by target, 1991–2000).

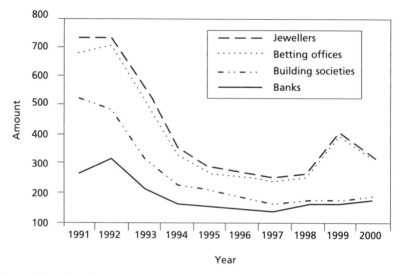

Source: Flying Squad: London

criminologists and policy-makers. Robbery decreased by over 30 per cent in the USA between 1993 and 1998, with a significant reduction in the use of firearms in the commissioning of these offences (Wintemunte 2000). The reasons for this unexpected decrease have been the subject of considerable speculation in the USA and have included changes in access and use of firearms, the incapacitation effect of imprisonment, changes in urban relations, changing patterns of drug use and the development of new styles of policing, as well as demographic changes (Blumstein and Wallman 2000).

Taking commercial robbery as our main point of reference, some of these competing explanations will be examined. In the course of the review we will draw upon some of the findings presented in previous chapters as well as considering additional contemporary material. Among the issues to be examined are the effectiveness of crime prevention measures, changes in the use of firearms, changing patterns of victimisation and developments in policing and sentencing policy, as well as more general changes in the nature of violence.

Crime prevention measures

It is inconceivable that, given the millions of pounds and dollars spent on crime prevention measures over the last two or three decades, these measures have not had some effect on the number of commercial robberies and on the way in which they are carried out. In many cases these measures can be seen to have an immediate effect in preventing robberies but there are also cases in which the introduction of crime prevention and crime reduction measures has been much more limited than is often assumed. In certain cases these measures have been counterproductive.

Most of the strategies that have been introduced to prevent or reduce armed robberies have involved various target-hardening strategies, mainly in the form of screens, alarms, double security doors and the like. It has been suggested these measures are likely to lead to a change of target or to escalation. The piecemeal and selective ways in which they have often been introduced may protect certain targets while leaving others vulnerable. In some instances prospective robbers have been encouraged to develop adaptive strategies. Target hardening draws mainly upon a mixture of commonsense notions of crime prevention, rational choice theory and routine activities theory. While the value of 'common sense' is often over-rated, rational choice theory, is it has been suggested, offers a limited approach to crime prevention mainly because it is not a 'theory' of offender motivation but, rather, involves a series of largely unsubstantiated propositions about how targets might be defended. For this reason it might be more accurately described as 'rational defence theory'. Moreover, its presumption of the 'rationality' of armed robbers is both exaggerated and largely misplaced. It makes little sense to attempt to understand the motivations of armed robbers within a simple rational/irrational opposition (Hindess 1988). There is a need for a deeper understanding of offender motivation and the often ambiguous and contradictory meanings that are attached to money, violence and drugs as well as to notions of masculinity (Messerschmidt 1993).

The routine activities perspective is no more helpful in understanding issues of motivation since its central presupposition that, for a crime to occur it requires a motivated offender, an appropriate target and a lack of adequate guardians begs the questions of what is meant by 'motivation', what constitutes an 'appropriate' target and what are 'adequate' guardians. Consequently, on all these critical points the routine activities approach is conspicuously silent and it ultimately dissolves into a series of platitudes (Ekblom and Tilley 2000).

The most useful and effective approaches, it has been argued, are those that attempt to grasp the inner logic of the robbery and, particularly, the need for the robber to gain 'control'. Strategies that increase uncertainty and introduce contingencies into this situation are likely to be most effective. These uncertainties can be maximised through internal design, by limiting the robber's range of vision, by dropping to the floor, by arranging the distribution and visibility of staff and by employing delaying tactics. Clearly the 'target hardening' measures, such as reducing the amount of cash available, will provide a disincentive to some robbers but these measures in themselves are clearly limited and may lead to increased frustration on the part of the robbers and to the subsequent escalation of violence.

Looking back over the last decade there is no clearly identifiable crime prevention strategy that has been introduced since 1993 into the UK that could reasonably account for the recorded reduction in commercial robberies. It might be possible to argue that it was not one specific measure that triggered this decrease but, rather, a culmination of tactics that worked in combination to reduce armed robberies. This proposal has a certain plausibility but the decrease in robberies amongst those targets that remain relatively unprotected makes this argument less than convincing and indicates the answer lies elsewhere.

As a number of commentators have noted, the notion of displacement remains a key concept in considering crime prevention and crime reduction strategies, but it remains poorly theorised and is notoriously difficult to measure (Gabor 1990; Barr and Pease 1990). However, the available evidence from the UK, Switzerland, Australia and Canada indicates that displacement has taken place within the commercial sector, with a shift towards the more vulnerable branches or sectors as a result of crime prevention interventions accompanied by changes in the modus operandi of robbers. Thus while there is evidence of a decrease in the number of robberies directed at those targets that have been given greater protection, it is often the case there is no noticeable decrease in the industry as a whole.

It was one of the central hypothesises of the research that we carried out that the recorded decrease in robberies against Band 1 targets would probably be associated with an increase in the generally more vulnerable Band 2 targets. This hypotheses was based on the assumption that the most likely form displacement would take would be a shift towards other, less well protected commercial targets. During the late 1980s and early 1990s in England and Wales, this hypothesis looked reasonably credible as the number of Band 1 robberies around the country declined steadily and the number of attacks against shops, garages, off-licences and similar premises started to increase. However, the decline in armed robberies against both Band 1 and Band 2 targets since 1993 has undermined the plausibility of this hypothesis and suggests that, if it is taking place between different types of premises, it is relatively limited or that it is taking other, less visible forms. The more plausible explanation is that the attractiveness of commercial robbery has decreased, particularly amongst the more professional criminals and that old-style 'blaggers' are diminishing in number; the newer recruits, on the other hand, are generally more desperate, disorganised and volatile offenders who are increasingly impervious to the distribution of crime prevention measures but who do not have the capacity to attack the more secure targets. At the same time the more experienced and generally older robbers appear to be moving into those areas of criminal activity that promise to be more lucrative, particularly those associated with drugs. The net effect of different forms of displacement and the changing motivations of armed robbers is reflected in changes in the use of weapons.

The availability and use of firearms

The impact of gun control strategies on the availability and use of firearms is difficult to determine since it is the pool of illegal firearms that will usually condition the choice of weapon. However, one of the notable shifts in the use of firearms in the UK in relation to armed robberies is that away from shotguns and towards handguns while, overall, there has been a decrease in the proportion of commercial robberies that involve firearms. This change in the choice of weapon, however, appears to be linked more to changes in the profile of offenders and to changes in style and the choice of target rather than to changes in gun control. It should also be noted that a considerable percentage of armed robberies involve other weapons besides firearms, and that in the majority of cases in which 'firearms' are reported to have been used they are either unloaded or are not capable of firing a lethal shot (Yardley and Maybanks 1992; Morrison and O'Donnell 1994). This observation has important implications for the meaning of 'armed' robbery. It suggests the term 'armed' needs to be deconstructed critically and that some distinction needs to be made in both analytic and policy terms between the type of weapon used and its potential and actual impact.

Although the stringent gun-control legislation that has been introduced in recent years into the UK cannot be shown to have had a direct effect on the availability and use of firearms, there is some evidence it has limited the pool of illegal weapons. The available research also suggests that a good proportion of these firearms are recycled and reactivated weapons and that many are old and unreliable (Bryan 1999). The contention that the majority of illegal firearms are imported, particularly from eastern Europe, that was promoted for some time by the media appears to be largely unfounded. The seizures of guns by HM Customs & Excise and the identification of those guns used in such offences as armed robbery suggest most firearms-related crime involves weapons that are already in circulation, have been acquired illegally from gun dealers or have been stolen. It also appears that the pool of illegal firearms is considerably smaller in the UK than is often suggested, and that the widely circulated figure of one million illegal firearms is a gross exaggeration. The reported increase in the use of replica firearms (and even toy guns) in the pursuit of robbery is indicative of the changing nature of 'armed' robbery. It also indicates that a growing proportion of commercial robbers do not have the time, organisation, funds or contacts to acquire real firearms.

American research on firearms paints a similar picture, although there are considerable differences in scale. As in the UK not only is the number of firearms-related robberies in decline but also the number of firearms-related offences in general has decreased over the last decade (Wintemunte 2000). The decrease in robbery and other forms of firearms-related crime in the USA is difficult to attribute in any direct way to changes in gun-control measures since firearms are so widely available and the pool of both legal and illegal firearms is so extensive. Claims that targeted intervention aimed at getting guns off the street, coupled with greater control of gun suppliers, may have had some effect on gun-related crimes in certain areas have some plausibility. However, the decreases that have been recorded in the USA in recent years appear relatively unrelated to changes in the regulation of firearms. The evidence from both sides of the Atlantic suggests it is not the case that those robbers who, five years ago, were robbing banks and building societies have now switched to more vulnerable targets and have adapted their weapon use accordingly. Rather, there has been a change in the profile of those engaged in commercial robberies. It is indicative that, while the growth of attacks against small retail outlets between 1985 and 1993 in the UK paralleled the changing balance of gun use from shotguns to handguns, the subsequent decrease in the number of attacks against retail outlets during the 1990s was not associated with any discernible change in weapon use at that time.

The use of guns by the police is an important element in the equation. The recent decision amongst the British police to remain 'unarmed' has almost certainly been conducive to the decreased use of firearms by commercial robbers. The experimentation with a new generation of less lethal weapons (including electrical stun guns and laser guns) is likely to reduce future demands for the British police to be routinely issued with firearms and should serve to maintain the de-escalation in the use of firearms amongst offenders, as well as limiting the development of a 'gun culture' in the UK.

The problematic nature of the concept of 'armed' in relation to commercial robberies calls into question the logic and appropriateness of current sentencing policy, which fails to make a clear distinction between the different forms of 'armed robbery'. Much of the justification for the relatively undifferentiated response to different types of commercial robbery involving different weapons is that the impact on the victim is largely the same since the victim at the moment of the robbery is unlikely to be able to distinguish between a real or imitation firearm and, therefore, is likely to suffer the same degree of trauma in either case. This policy, it has been argued, is short sighted and inequitable and does little to reduce the threat to future victims since there is little disincentive for the robber to carry an unloaded or imitation firearm. The present sentencing policy for armed robbers appears, on both sides of the Atlantic, to be directed primarily towards the protection of property interests rather than the protection of persons.

The changing patterns of victimisation

Despite the growing preoccupation in criminological circles with different forms of victimisation, the personal victims of armed robbery remain a much neglected group, despite the high level of trauma they are known to experience. The decrease in the number of commercial robberies has been welcome news to the staff who work in commercial premises although, for those who remain victims, the overall decrease in the level of personal and organisational victimisation provides little comfort. Moreover, the decrease in victimisation has not been evenly spread in England and Wales across different types of target. The most dramatic decreases in recent years have taken place in banks and building societies, which arguably provide the best available level of training and support to the staff who have experienced an armed robbery, although it is evident that the degree of support offered by different firms varies considerably (Bains and Richards 1998). Implicit in a number of reports produced by the Health and Safety Executive 1993; Standing and Nicolini 1997) and the like is that there is a consensus of interests between the staff and management of these institutions and that little consideration is given to the competing interests involved in terms of responsibility, security and compensation. One indication of this conflict of interests is the increasing adoption of open-plan designs, particularly in banks and building societies, which are seen by these organisations as being more user friendly although they tend to increase the exposure of staff to danger.

Whatever the limitations may be of the support provided by different banks and building societies, it is evident the staff in small retail outlets generally receive much less support. A considerable percentage of armed robberies against commercial establishments takes place after 6 p.m. in shops, fast-food outlets, off-licences and convenience stores. Many of these premises are staffed by untrained, low-paid staff who are exposed to robbers who may be desperate and unpredictable. The uncertainty of the event tends to make the experience of robbery even more traumatic. Employees, however, are often encouraged to carry on as if nothing had happened and a significant percentage who suffer long-term trauma have little option but to change their jobs, if they can. Many robbers whom we interviewed said they sought out young female staff who, they felt, were most vulnerable and least likely to resist, although in a number of cases they were surprised by the responses of female staff. What is clear is that victimisation is not random. Rather, it is patterned and, to some degree, predictable.

One of the best predictors of whether a premises was likely to be victimised was whether it had been victimised in the past. Our data on banks and building societies in the London area revealed that 41 per cent of building society branches had been victimised more than once between 1992 and 1994, while 35 per cent of banks had been victimised over the same period. Further research might reveal whether the decrease in armed robberies is connected to changes in the number and frequency of repeats.

A considerable percentage of staff who experienced armed robberies put up some form of resistance and demonstrated that victimisation is, ultimately, a negotiated status, albeit in a situation involving an asymmetrical balance of power. Victim resistance can take a number of forms, and the response of victims can be critical in influencing the outcome of the robbery, the amount taken and the probability of the robber being caught and prosecuted. Although these actions may have been influential in particular cases and some organisations have undoubtedly reduced the level of successful robberies against their branches by training their staff to drop to the floor, to delay in the handing over money or to fill bags with notes of small denominations, it is difficult to see how these forms of victim resistance could have instigated a general decrease in armed robbery in different types of premises. A more promising explanation for the decrease in armed robbery is more commonly seen as being associated with changes in the nature of policing.

The impact of policing and sentencing strategies

There can be little doubt that the overall impact of policing during the 1980s and early 1990s in England and Wales had the effect of reducing the number of career criminals who were involved in commercial robberies. Clear-up rates averaging over 30 per cent in a number of forces meant it was probable that the more persistent armed robbers were being caught by one method or another and that this must have had a depressing effect on the number of armed robberies carried out during this period. The exceptionally long sentences that tend to be meted out to those convicted of armed robbery ensured that, once convicted of this offence, the vast majority of robbers are imprisoned for a considerable length of time. The incapacitation effect of existing sentencing policy has almost certainly been more effective in reducing robberies than the deterrent effect, except for some of the older robbers who, at a certain point in their lives, decide that the possibility of a 10 or 15-year stretch outweighs the probable gains from armed robbery.

However, as we have seen in relation to the Flying Squad, the clear-up rate began to decline precisely at the point when armed robbery against commercial premises began to decrease. Significantly, armed robberies against such Band 2 targets as shops and garages in the London area also decreased, despite the fact the Flying Squad had little or no involvement with these type of robberies at the time.

The pressure for the police to develop more proactive and intelligence-led policing strategies by both the Audit Commission and the Home Office appears to be largely misplaced, not only in relation to armed robbery but also in relation to other offences such as burglary (Stockdale and Gresham 1998). Although the terms 'proactive' and 'intelligence led' suggests an approach that involves acting faster and thinking smarter, the reality is that it becomes a less appropriate strategy as the number of Band 1 robberies decreases and the number of 'known' suspects at large dwindles. It is for this reason that the longer-term viability of a dedicated unit such as the Flying Squad focusing exclusively on Band 1 targets has been called into question.

All good police work involves the gathering and analysis of information, whether it be categorised as 'reactive' or 'proactive'. As the number of professional and 'known' armed robbers continues to decline in the UK, there needs to be greater co-ordination between patrol officers (who are often the first to arrive at the scene of the crime) and detectives (who are charged with developing an appropriate response). The role of detective work and, particularly, the development of effective interviewing and interrogation skills should be promoted rather than paying lip service to the deployment of proactive strategies or relying on technological devices.

Although it may be claimed that the relatively long sentences handed out to those convicted of armed robbery may have had the effect of taking a number of persistent armed robbers out of circulation, current sentencing strategies also incur considerable costs in terms of locking up other types of offenders for long periods. This strategy can serve to establish minor offenders in their criminal careers while creating injustices by failing to distinguish clearly between those who carry a loaded lethal firearm and those who do not. By adopting such a policy British courts fail to distinguish between the hardened robbers who are prepared to use a loaded weapon if considered necessary and those who carry plastic weapons or cucumbers or bananas. In this way the courts misinterpret the seriousness of the offence and disregard considerations of proportionality.

In sum, policing and sentencing strategies have had a discernible effect upon armed robbery, albeit at a price. However, the dramatic decrease in recorded commercial robberies in England and Wales since 1993 does not appear to be linked directly with the changing styles of policing or sentencing policy. As Shona Morrison and Ian O'Donnell (1994) conclude in their study of armed robbery in London: 'neither the prospect of eventual arrest and a lengthy term of imprisonment, nor increased target hardening, appeared to be given much weight during the planning and execution of these offences.'

Changing motivation and modus operandi

The most noticeable change that has occurred over the last decade has been the demise of the more professional and career robbers and, subsequently, a greater proportion of those currently involved in commercial robbery are more inexperienced, younger, more desperate, more criminally diverse and more spontaneous in their actions. The emerging commercial robbers do not aspire to become like the old-time 'blaggers' and 'faces' who identified and surveyed possible targets, gathered the necessary equipment and planned their getaways. The contemporary armed robber is more likely to be more spontaneous and desperate. One notable example of the changing nature of commercial robberies is for a gang to 'steam' into a retail outlet, jump across the counter and clean out the till. They may not even carry weapons but rely on the element of surprise and the weight of numbers to carry out the robbery.

For many of these offenders robbery is part of a diverse repertoire of offending. Commercial robbery represents just one option in a rich array of criminal opportunities. Indicatively, recent reports from the Flying Squad in London suggest that over 20 per cent of recorded commercial robberies in London involved 'steaming'. Associated with this change in the modus operandi is a change in the selection of targets in the Metropolitan Police District, with late-night shops, convenience stores and fast-food outlets increasingly becoming the targets of robbery (see Table 7.2).

Table 7.2: Commercial robberies falling within the Flying Squad terms of reference (1991–2000).

	Cash-in-transit	Banks	Post offices	Building societies	Betting offices	Jewellers	Other premises	Total
1991	230	327	126	529	317	89		1,618
1992	154	433	165	325	447	54		1,578
1993	138	232	148	210	402	63		1,193
1994	103	128	84	115	221	28		679
1995	126	100	101	111	131	28		597
1996	148	92	104	69	167	16		596
1997	189	66	126	40	167	20	244	852
1998	156	122	71	19	177	21	434	1,000
1999	148	114	136	21	444	36	471	1,370
2000	242	152	114	19	242	31	532	1,332

Source: Information supplied by the Flying Squad Crime Prevention Unit.

As Dick Hobbs (1995) has argued, we are currently witnessing the mutation of the professional criminal as a consequence of the changes that are taking place in the structures of the illegitimate markets, as well as associated changes in cultural sensibilities. Just as the skills of old-time professional craft criminals became obsolete and were superseded by a new generation of career criminals popularly associated with the Krays, the Richardsons and the Great Train Robbers in the UK, these groups of professional criminals themselves appear increasingly anachronistic. Thus:

What has been traditionally defined as professional crime has now fragmented into a number of quite distinctive forms of criminality. The decline of the key criminal activities that were previously central to the concept of professional crime into haphazard, essentially amateur excursions, featuring minimal planning, a low level of competence, and a lack of commitment to specialised criminality, typifies contemporary armed robbery and stands in stark contrast to the teams of robbers whose competent practice was efficient enough to establish 'blaggers' as a criminal elite (Hobbs 1995: 9).

The changes that are currently underway not only represent a decrease in the number of recorded commercial robberies but also the demise of the armed robber as a career criminal. If this trend continues, the image of the balaclava-clad villain wielding a sawn-off shot-gun and demanding money at the counter will be the subject of media productions. An examination of current trends suggests that the complex changes in the types of offenders who are currently involved in armed robbery – and the changing nature of commercial robbery itself – can be seen as a function of four inter-related developments that have been gathering pace in the UK in recent years: deskilling, democratisation, diversification and disarming.

Deskilling

Since the 1950s we can identify three phases in the development of commercial robbery that involve the gradual deskilling of this activity. In the immediate postwar period commercial robberies were predominantly 'craft' crimes that involved the use of technical skills to crack open a safe or, in some cases, robbers used a thermic lance. During the 1970s and 1980s there was a shift towards 'project' crime that typically involved several robbers attacking a target with a weapon, normally a firearm. While project crime frequently involved some degree of planning and organisation, the familiar scenario of robbers entering the premises and threatening counter staff with a club or a firearm required little expertise. Increasingly, as firearms became more widely employed, the level of planning decreased and the number of unsuccessful robberies increased as robbers relied on the authority of the gun to carry them through (Ekblom 1987).

Over the last decade or so there are indications that an increasing proportion of commercial robberies are becoming more spontaneous events with limited planning and expertise. A growing number of robbers appear desperate and disorganised and are only prepared to attack 'soft' targets. In general they have lower expectations of potential rewards from robbery.

Democratisation

Closely associated with deskilling is the increasing democratisation of commercial robberies. The demise of the old elite of professional armed robbers has made it an offence open to a wider group of offenders. Amongst this group there is less deference to the known 'faces', and the use of violence appears to be becoming more spontaneous and, at times, more gratuitous.

There is less need for criminal expertise, and less emulation of established figures and practices. Anyone who is desperate or brave enough can take his chance. For those who have little or nothing to lose, the prospect of quick cash, however minimal it might be, is increasingly attractive. Money is for immediate consumption and the instant satisfaction of cravings and desires. The objective is not to build up a 'stash' of money to purchase weapons and materials for future robberies or to pay people off. Instead, the contemporary robber is more likely to 'earn and burn' the money.

Diversification

The process of diversification in relation to armed robbery is taking a number of different forms. First, there is growing evidence that many of the more experienced robbers are diversifying into other forms of illegitimate entrepeneurship, particularly the importation and selling of drugs and the financing of drug deals. A number of robbers we interviewed told us they were carrying out armed robberies to finance drugs deals in which they generally expected to double their initial investment. As one commentator put it, armed robbery in the last decade has become 'dangerous and unfashionable' while 'the profits from the drugs trade dwarf the proceeds of all but the biggest robberies', and these proceeds 'can be concealed or laundered far more readily than identifiable bank notes or bullion' (Rose 1988). Some of those we interviewed in prison stated they were going to take up drug dealing on release, since they felt this was a more lucrative and safer activity. However, amongst those who had become involved with drug dealing, there was some misgivings about how their lives had changed in that they had become increasingly paranoid as a result of the real possibility of being 'ripped off' by other villains. They pointed out that, because the money from the armed robberies was immediately invested in illicit drugs, the 'good times' that had once followed on from successful robbery were now being deferred. The balance between the pursuit of hedonism and 'doing the business' was shifting.

Amongst the intermediates, drug dealing (normally at a lower level) is regularly combined with a diverse range of criminal activity. This group may well combine robberies with burglaries and other forms of theft as opportunities arise. They do not for the most part identify themselves as 'armed robbers': they are criminal diversifiers prepared to turn their hand to any activity that is attractive and potentially lucrative.

Amongst the more inexperienced amateurs the forms of diversification are a little different in that their commitment to crime is normally less developed and more sporadic. Consequently, armed robbery may occupy a peripheral place in their lives and, apart from periods of desperation in which their involvement in armed robbery may be intense but often short lived, they are less involved in crime, except possibly the use and sale of illicit drugs. Thus the important distinction between these amateurs and the intermediate group is that the formers' lives have not become centred around criminal activities. In the language of criminology they remain primary rather than secondary deviants and have not, as yet, come to identify themselves as full-time criminals.

Disarming

The decrease in the use of firearms in recent years is surprising since there is a sense that firearms use and random killings are on the increase. Dramatic media reports in the UK of homicides as a result of random or professional 'hitmen' together with a number of high-profile shootings, give the impression that fatalities resulting from the use of firearms are rising. This picture is underpinned by a widely held view we are becoming a more violent society. Against this background the reported decrease in the use of firearms, particularly sawn-off shotguns and rifles, is surprising. However, the change to handguns, pistols and imitation weapons is indicative of the changing nature of those who currently engage in armed robbery. Handguns are more fashionable and flexible and can be easily carried on the person and they are, therefore, more readily available for use when the appropriate situation arises.

It is also the case, as we have noted, that a significant percentage of firearms are not real or not capable of firing a lethal shot. However, the indications are the use of imitation or unloaded weapons is on the increase while it is also evident that a growing percentage of commercial robberies do not involve the use of threat of firearms as such but rely on surprise and physical intimidation.

These four related trends signify a substantial change in the nature of commercial robbery in the UK, such that the term 'armed robbery' appears to be an increasingly inaccurate way of classifying these offences. The term 'robbery' has always been problematic and the time has come to reclassify offences against commercial and non-commercial targets and to distinguish more clearly between those that involve real working firearms that are loaded and those that do not.

The changing nature of (male) violence

The fact that commercial robbery is decreasing in both the USA and Britain suggests it might be associated with broader cultural changes in attitudes towards violence in its various forms. Moreover, recent changes in the nature and level of armed robbery appear to transcend periods of high and low employment and are largely impervious to changing political leadership. Since changes in crime prevention, policing, victim resistance and gun use do not fully account for recent developments, this suggests we need to locate the recorded decreases in commercial robbery within a wider explanatory framework (Rosenfield 2000). Our examination of a changing offender motivation, modus operandi and profile of commercial robbers suggests a change of sensibilities is occurring amongst the new generation of commercial robbers, and that these may well reflect changing social attitudes towards violence.

It might be expected in countries that are becoming more market orientated and decreasingly regulated by welfare mechanisms that violence in its various forms would increase (Currie 1997). The destruction of traditional forms of employment, the fragmentation of communities and the consequent erosion of informal and communal networks have all been identified as contributing to the growth of violent crime. However, despite the considerable evidence that these processes are well under way, the consequent growth in violent crime has not occurred in either the USA or Britain. To be sure, certain forms of violence are being recorded at increasing levels, but the relentless increase in all forms of violent crime some criminologists had predicted has failed to materialise. It is also the case that a significant percentage of the recorded increase in a number of forms of violence (such as rape, domestic violence and child abuse) is a function of increased reporting rates rather than an increase in the incidence of these offences. Because armed robbery has a relatively high level of reporting and recording, the reductions that have been noted are based on what is widely considered to be 'hard data' and, therefore, these recent changes are particularly worthy of investigation.

What is of interest here are not only the levels of recorded crimes of violence (such as armed robbery) but also the ways in which the expressions of violence itself are changing, particularly amongst the young. There seems to be a move away in recent times from organised violence in the forms of football hooliganism and gang warfare in the UK towards more spontaneous and gratuitous expressions of violence. These new developments appear to be linked to changing community and family relations and the emergence of new forms of individualism and collectivism (Bauman 1995; Maffesoli 1996). In particular, we are witnessing changing forms of gender identity as traditional notions of masculinity come under pressure and as young males are identified increasingly as consumers and spenders rather than as workers and providers.

As Beatrice Campbell (1993) has argued, the changing nature of the crimes perpetrated by young males is not so much a response to unemployment as an attempt to reassert notions of masculinity in a world of changing gender relations. As she puts it, the reassertion of masculinity amongst the 'underclass' involves a number of elements, including having 'bottle', stealing, looking for fights, being a bit crazier than everybody else and being able to get control of other people. Recent accounts of disorder and crime in inner-city streets at weekends involving heavy drinking identify a similar set of priorities amongst a cross-section of young people (Hobbs *et al* 2000).

The ways in which these changes are manifesting themselves in relation to commercial robbery are that attacks appear to be more spontaneous, involving young people propelled by drugs and alcohol in search of excitement. The new generation of commercial robbers is tied increasingly to consumerism, excitement and the need to engage in risk activities in a world that is becoming more fragmented and alienating. Indicatively, whereas the old-style robbers referred to robberies as 'pieces of work' or 'graft', the new recruits tend increasingly see it as a 'buzz' and approach robberies in a state of both desperation and anticipation. The new generation see robbery and other forms of crime as a constituent part of a pattern of consumption and of heightened experiences and extravagant pleasures. Within this lifestyle, drug use becomes a normalised part of everyday life. It is not so much a form of pathology or a problem to be overcome but may, as Jack Katz (1988) has argued, provide an organising theme in their otherwise chaotic lives. Drug taking, like armed robbery, creates the space for some young men to act out predatory forms of masculinity. Engaging in serious drug use, like engaging in armed robbery, involves a test of masculinity and it provides another form of risk-taking; it forms part of a pattern of conspicuous consumption while demonstrating the ability to be 'mad' or 'bad' (Auld *et al* 1986). The term 'edgework' has been used to capture the response to and adaption by a number of young people of the cultural and economic constraints of late modernity (Lyng 1993; Ferrell *et al* 2001):

Edgework represents a sometimes spontaneous search for a dramatic self within a world of alienation and over-socialisation. Being on the edge, or over it – beyond reason and in passion – is momentarily to grasp a spiritual and romantic utopia (Collison 1996: 435).

The buzz and sense of control that are widely referred to by armed robbers are a critical part of the process. The robbery provides a momentary sense of power in an overdetermined world of exclusion and marginalisation. Armed robbery combines in one act the possibility of moving beyond reason, embracing risk, taking control and acquiring the means for engaging in extravagant forms of consumption.

The form of robbery that has continued to increase in the UK is street robbery. In our interviews with convicted armed robbers in the early 1990s it was apparent there was a relatively clear distinction between those who selected commercial targets and those who attacked people on the street. In the eyes of the majority of commercial robbers, street robbers were 'scum', and the techniques of neutralisation they employed did not extend to personal victims. However, in the current period an overlap can be detected between the new generation of commercial robbers and street robbers. Both forms of robbery involve little planning and the selection of accessible and vulnerable targets for relatively small rewards. Thus it is the case that the differences in terms of motivation, expertise and objectives are becoming increasingly blurred (Barker *et al* 1993).

Conclusion

The available evidence indicates we are witnessing the demise of the professional 'armed' robbery and of armed robbery as a criminal career. In its place are emerging new modes of taking money by using threats or force. The profile of those engaged in armed robbery is changing, as are the methods by which robberies are carried out. These developments present new problems for the control of robbery. The police are less able to rely on strategies that involve rounding up the usual suspects; instead they have the task of gathering information and intelligence on a diverse range of offenders whose commitment to robbery is variable and often short lived. In this changing situation, the emphasis on proactive policing is largely misplaced as are the notions that the typical armed robber is a persistent and rational offender.

Alongside changes in the nature of policing, changes in sentencing policy are called for. The downsizing and disarming of a significant percentage of those currently engaged in 'armed robbery' raise the issue of the meaning of the term 'armed'. Distinctions need to be made amongst sentencers between those carrying lethal weapons and those who do not. A rational sentencing policy would provide every incentive for prospective robbers not to carry loaded weapons and to avoid the use of violence in general.

There are a number of costs and benefits associated with these recent developments. The demise of the shotgun-wielding 'blagger' will mean the number of attacks against the larger financial institutions will be likely to continue decreasing. At the same time the growing proportion of less experienced commercial robbers will probably increase the number of failed and aborted attacks. Changes in the composition of commercial robbers will also have a depressing effect on the average amount of money stolen, while the increased use of replica and implied weapons suggests victims may be less traumatised as the lethality of the weapons used decreases. On the downside, a significant percentage of the new generation of robbers are more unpredictable and generally more desperate. Often fuelled by drink and drugs, they are more likely to engage in gratuitous violence, particularly when they confront victims who resist handing over the money.

We have entered a new era of crime and crime control in which the changing nature and response to armed robbery need to be understood. The motivation and objectives of those engaging in commercial robbery are in the process of transformation, such that the images and explanations we have employed in the past look increasingly anachronistic. We are being forced to rethink the key concepts of violence, risk and dangerousness if we are to develop responses to robbery that are both effective and appropriate.

References

Addley, E. (2001) Less lethal police arms tested. *Guardian* 17 April.

Albanese, J. (1989) *Organised Crime in America.* Cincinnati, OH: Anderson.

Audit Commission (1990) *Effective Policing – Performance Review in Police Forces.* London: HMSO.

Audit Commission (1993) *Helping with Enquiries: Tackling Crime Effectively.* London: HMSO.

Audit Commission (1996) *Detecting a Change: Progress in Tackling Crime.* London: HMSO.

Auld, J., Dorn, N. and South, N. (1986) Irregular work, irregular pleasures: heroin in the 1980s. In R. Matthews and J. Young (eds.) *Confronting Crime.* London: Sage.

Austin, C. (1988) *The Prevention of Robbery in Building Society Branches. Crime Prevention Unit Paper 14.* London: Home Office.

Bachman, R. (1996) Victims' perceptions of initial police response to robbery and aggravated assault: does race matter? *Journal of Quantitative Criminology* 12(4): 363–90.

Bains, J. and Richards, D. (1998) *The Impact of Armed Robberies on Employees Working in Financial Institutions.* The Longlarten Research Trust.

Ball, J., Chester, L. and Perrot, R. (1978) *Cops and Robbers: An Investigation into Armed Bank Robberies.* London: Deutsch.

Banking Insurance and Finance Union (1994) *Armed Raids: Bank and Building Society Branches.* London: BIFU.

Banton, M. (1985) *Investigating Robbery.* Aldershot: Gower.

Baril, M. and Morissette, A. (1985) From the perspective of victims: another point of view on armed robbery. *Criminology* 18(2): 117–37.

Barker, M., Geraghty, J., Webb, B. and Key, T. (1993) *The Prevention of Street Robbery. Crime Prevention Unit Series Paper 44.* London: Home Office.

Barr, R. and Pease, K. (1990) Crime placement, displacement and deflection. In N. Morris and M. Tonry (eds.) *Crime and Justice: A Review of Research*. Chicago, IL: University of Chicago Press.

Bauman, Z. (1995) *Life in Fragments: Essays in Postmodern Morality*. Oxford: Blackwell.

Bayley, D. (1994) *Police for the Future*. New York: Oxford University Press.

Bellamy, L. (1995) *Situational Crime Prevention Strategies for Combating Convenience Store Robbery*. New Brunswick, NJ: Rutgers University Press.

Bennett, T. (2000) *Drugs and Crime: The Results of the Second Developmental Stage of the NEW-ADAM programme*. Research Study 205. London: Development and Statistics Directorate, Home Office.

Bennetto, J. (1994) The police seek wider use of armed patrols. *The Independent* 8 July.

Bhaskar, R. (1975) *A Realist Theory of Science*. Brighton: Harvester.

Blumstein, A. (1994) Youth violence, guns and the illicit drug industry. *The Journal of Criminal Law and Criminology* 86(1): 10–36.

Blumstein, A. and Wallman, J. (2000) The recent rise and fall of American violence. In A. Blumstein and J. Wallman (eds.) *The Crime Drop in America*. New York: Cambridge University Press.

Bottomley, K. and Coleman, C. (1995) The police. In M. Walker (ed.) *Interpreting Crime Statistics*. Oxford: Clarendon Press.

Bourgois, P. (1996) In search of masculinity: violence, respect and sexuality among Puerto Rican crack cocaine dealers in Harlem. *British Journal of Criminology* 36(3): 412–48.

British Retail Consortium (1999) *Retail Crime Survey 1999*. London: HMSO.

Brooks, C. and Cross, C. (1996) *Retail Crime Costs 1994/5 Survey*. London: British Retail Consortium.

Brown, J. (1996) Police research: some critical issues. In F. Leishman *et al* (eds.) *Core Issues in Policing*. London: Longman.

Bryan, J. (2000) *Illegal Firearms in the United Kingdom*. London: The Centre for Defence Studies, King's College.

Budd, T. (1999) *Violence at Work: Findings from the British Crime Survey*. London: Home Office.

Burney, E. (1990) *Putting Street Crime in its Place. A Report to the Community/ Police Consultative Group for Lambeth*. London: Centre For Inner City Studies, Goldsmiths College.

Calder, J. and Bauer, J. (1992) Convenience store robberies: security measures and store robbery incidents. *Journal of Criminal Justice* 20: 553–66.

Campbell, B. (1993) *Goliath: Britain's Dangerous Places*. London: Methuen.

Campbell, D. (1994) Strong-arm men. *Guardian*, 23 March.

Campbell, D. (1998) Police suspended in corruption raids. *Guardian* 28 January.

Carroll, R. and Dodd, V. (2000) Knightsbridge robber baron dies in shootout. *Guardian* 19 April.

Challinger, D. (ed.) (1989) *Armed Robbery: Proceedings of a Seminar*. Canberra: Australian Institute of Criminology.

Chatterton, M. (1987) Assessing police effectiveness – future prospects. *British Journal of Criminology* 27(1): 80–86.

Cherryman, J. and Bull, R. (2000) Reflections on investigative interviewing. In F. Leishman *et al* (eds.) *Core Issues in Policing* (2nd edn). Harlow: Pearson Education.

Clarke, M. (1994) Time for a change. *Police Review* 14 January.

Clarke, R. (ed.) (1997) *Situational Crime Prevention: Successful Case Studies* (2nd edn). New York: Harrow & Heston.

Clarke, R. (2001) Informers and corruption. In R. Billingsley, T. Nemitz and P. Bean (eds.) *Informers: Policing, Policy and Practice*. Cullompton: Willan.

Clarke, R., Field, S., and McGrath, G. (1990) Target hardening of banks in Australia and displacement of robberies. *Security Journal* 2(2): 84–90.

Clarke, R. and McGrath, G. (1990) Cash reduction and robbery prevention in Australian betting shops. *Security Journal* 1(3): 160–63.

Clarke, R. and Weisburd, D. (1994) Diffusion of crime control benefits: observations on the reverse of displacement. *Crime Prevention Studies* 2: 165–83.

Cohen, L., Cantor, D. and Kluegel, J. (1981) Robbery victimisation in the US: an analysis of a non-random event. *Social Science Quarterly* 62(4): 644–57.

Cohen, L. and Felson, M. (1979) Social change and crime trends. A routine activity approach. *American Sociological Review* 44: 588–608.

Collison, M. (1996) In search of the high life: drugs, crime, masculinities and consumption. *British Journal of Criminology* 36(3): 428–44.

Conklin, J. (1972) *Robbery and the Criminal Justice System*. New York: Lippincott.

Cook, P. (1976) A strategic choice analysis of robbery. In W. Skogan (ed.) *Sample Surveys of the Victims of Crime*. Cambridge, MA: Ballinger.

Cook, P. (1982) The role of firearms in violent crime – an interpretive review of the literature. In M. Wolfgang and N. Weiner (eds.) *Criminal Violence*. London: Sage.

Cook, P. (1983) *Robbery in the United States: An Analysis of Recent Trends and Patterns*. Washington, DC: National Institute of Justice.

Cook, P. (1987) Robbery violence. *Journal of Criminal Law and Criminology* 78: 357–76.

Cook, P. (1990) Robbery in the United States: an analysis of recent trends patterns. In N. Weiner *et al* (eds.) *Violence, Patterns, Causes, and Public Policy*. New York: Harcourt Brace.

Cook, P. (1991) The technology of personal violence. In M. Tonry (ed.) *Crime and Justice. Vol. 14*. Chicago, IL: University of Chicago Press.

Cook, P. and Laub, J. (1998) The unprecedented epidemic in youth violence. In M. Moore and M. Tonry (eds.) *Crime and Justice: A Review of Research*. Chicago, IL: University of Chicago Press.

Cook, P. and Moore, M. (1999) Guns, gun control and homicide. In M. Smith and M. Zhan (eds.) *Studying and Preventing Homicide: Issues and Challenges*. Thousand Oaks, CA: Sage.

Cooper, P. and Murphy, J. (1997) Ethical approaches for police officers when working with informants in the development of criminal intelligence in the United Kingdom. *Journal of Social Policy* 26(1): 1–20.

Cornish, D. and Clarke, R. (eds.) (1986) *The Reasoning Criminal: Rational Choice Perspectives on Offending*. New York: Springer-Verlag.

Cornish, D. and Clarke, R. (1987) Understanding crime displacement: an application of rational choice theory. *Criminology* 25(4): 933–47.

Creedon, M. (1992) Armed robbery in Leicestershire and Northampton-shire. MA thesis, University of Leicester.

Cukier, W and Shropshire, S. (2000) Domestic gun markets: licit and illicit links. In L. Lumpe (ed.) *Running Guns: The Global Black Market in Small Arms*. London: Zed Books.

Curie, E. (1997) Market, crime and community: towards a mid-range theory of post-industrial violence. *Theoretical Criminology* 1(2): 147–72.

Customs & Excise (1997) *Annual Report: The Protection of Society*. London: HMSO.

Darbyshire, N. and Hilliard, B. (1993) *The Flying Squad*. London: Headline.

Davis, N. (1999) Watching the detectives: how the police cheat in the fight against crime. *Guradian* 18 March.

Decker, S., Pennell, S. and Caldwell, A. (1997) *Illegal Firearms: Access and Use by Arrestees*. Washington, DC: National Institute of Justice.

Diaz, T. (1999) *Making a Killing: The Business of Guns in America*. New York: New Press.

Dorn, N., Murji, K. and South, N. (1992) *Traffickers: Drug Markets and Law Enforcement*. London: Routledge.

Duffala, D. (1976) Convenience stores armed robbery and physical environmental features. *American Behavioral Scientist* 20(20): 227–45.

Dunningham, C. and Norris, C. (1999) The detective, the snout and the

Audit Commission: the real cost of using informants. *The Howard Journal* 38(1): 67–86.

Eck, J. (1983) *Solving Crimes: The Investigation of Robbery and Burglary.* Washington, DC: Police Executive Research Forum, US Department of Justice.

Eck, J. (1992) Criminal investigation. In G. Cordner and D. Hale (eds.) *What Works in Policing?* Cincinnati, OH: Anderson Publishing.

Eck, J. and Maguire, M. (2000) Have changes in policing reduced violent crime? An assessment of evidence. In A. Blumstein and J. Wallman (eds.) *The Crime Drop in America.* New York: Cambridge University Press.

Ekblom, P. (1987) *Preventing Robberies at Sub-Post Offices: An Evaluation of a Security Initiative. Crime Prevention Unit Paper* 9. London: Home Office.

Ekblom, P. and Simon, F. (1988) *Crime and Racial Harassment in Asian Run Small Shops. Crime Prevention Unit Paper* 15. London: Home Office.

Ekblom, P. and Tilley, N. (2000) Going equipped: criminology, situational crime prevention and the resourceful offender. *British Journal of Criminology* 40: 376–98.

Ericson, R. and Haggerty, K. (1997) *Policing the Risk Society.* Oxford: Clarendon Press.

Farrell, G. and Pease, K. (1993) *Once Bitten, Twice Bitten: Repeat Vicitimisation and its Implications for Crime Prevention. Crime Prevention Unit Paper* 46. London: Home Office.

Feeney, F. and Weir, (1986) Robbers as decision makers. In D. Cornish and R. Clarke (eds.) *The Reasoning Criminal.* New York: Springer-Verlag.

Ferrell, J., Milovanovic, D. and Lyng, S. (2001) Edgework, media practices and the elongation of meaning. *Theoretical Criminology* 5(2): 177–201.

Flood-Paige, C. and Mackie, A. (1998) *Sentencing Practice: An Examination of Decisions in Magistrates Courts and the Crown Court in the Mid 1990's. Research Study* 180. London: HMSO.

Foster, J. (1990) *Villains: Crime and Community in the Inner City.* London: Routledge.

Fry, C. (1989) Dangerous imitations. *Police Review* 29 September: 1968–69.

Fry, C. (1991) Playing with fire. *Police Review* 13 September: 1850–1.

Gabor, T. (1989) Preventing armed robbery through opportunity reduction: a critical analysis. *Journal of Security Administration* 12(1) 13–18.

Gabor,T. (1990) Crime displacement and situational prevention. *Canadian Journal of Criminology* January: 41–73.

Gabor, T., Baril, M., Cusson, M., Elie, D., Leblanc, M. and Normandeau, A. (1987) *Armed Robbery: Cops, Robbers and Victims*. Springfield, IL: Charles Thomas.

Gagnon, R. and Leblanc, M. (1983) Police responses in armed robbery cases. *Canadian Police College Journal* 7(4): 297–310.

Genders, E. and Player, E. (1995) *Grendon: A Study of a Therapeutic Prison*. Oxford: Clarendon Press.

Gill, M. and Matthews, R. (1994) Robbers on robbery: offenders perspectives. In M. Gill (ed.) *Crime at Work*. Leicester: Perpetuity Press.

Gill, P. (2000) *Rounding up the Usual Suspects*. Aldershot: Ashgate.

Grandjean, C. (1990) Bank robberies and physical security in Switzerland: a case study of the escalation and displacement phenomena. *Security Journal* 1(3): 155–59.

Grant, L. (1992) Unprepared victims at the wrong end of a gun. The *Independent on Sunday* 5 April.

Greenwood, C. (1972) *Firearms Controls: A Study of Armed Crime and Firearms Control in England and Wales*. London: Routledge & Kegan Paul.

Greenwood, C. (1983) Armed crime: a declaration of war. *Security Gazette* June: 1071–75.

Greenwood, C. (1986) Yesterday's thieves, today's muggers: tomorrow's gunmen? *Police* January: 28–30.

Greer, S. (2001) Where the grass is greener? Supergrasses in comparative perspective. In R. Billingsly, T. Nemitz and P. Bean (eds.) *Informers: Policing, Policy and Practice*. Cullompton: Willan.

Hall, S., Critcher, C., Jefferson, T., Clarke, J. and Roberts, B. (1978) *Policing the Crisis: Mugging, the State and Law and Order*. London: Macmillan.

Hanvey, P. (1995) *Identifying, Recruiting and Handling Informers Paper 5*. London: Police Research Group: Home Office.

Harding, R. (1979) Firearms use in crime. *Criminal Law Review* 765–74.

Health and Safety Executive (1993) *Prevention of Violence to Staff in Banks and Building Societies*. London: HSE Books.

Heaton. R, (2000) The prospects for intellligence-led policing: some historical and quantitative considerations. *Policing and Society* 9: 337–55.

Hetherington, P. (1994) Doubts over armed officers despite gun crime rise. *Guardian* 17 May.

Hibberd, M. and Shapland, J. (1993) *Violent Crime in Small Shops*. London: Police Foundation.

Hindess, B. (1988) *Choice, Rationality and Social Theory*. London: Unwin Hyman.

Hobbs, D. (1989) *Doing the Business: Entrepreneurship, The Working Class, and Detectives in the East End of London*. Oxford: Oxford University Press.

Hobbs, D. (1995) *Bad Business: Professional Crime in Modern Britain*. Oxford: Oxford University Press.

Hobbs, D. (2000) Researching serious crime. In R. King and E. Wincup (eds.) *Doing Research on Crime and Justice*. Oxford: Oxford University Press.

Hobbs, D., Lister, S., Hadfield, D., Winlow, S. and Hall, S. (2000) Receiving shadows: governnance and liminality in the nightime economy. *British Journal of Sociology* 51(1): 701–17.

Holdaway, S. (1983) *Inside the British Police: A Force at Work*. Oxford: Blackwell.

Holmes, M., Daudistel, H. and Farrell, R. (1987) Determinants of charge reductions and final dispositions in cases of burglary and robbery. *Journal of Research in Crime and Delinquency* 24(3): 233–54.

Home Affairs Committee (2000) *Control over Firearms*. London: HMSO.

Home Office (1973) *The Control of Firearms in Britain: A Consultative Document*. London: HMSO.

Home Office (1986) *Standing Conference on Crime Prevention. Report of the Working Group on Commercial Robbery*. London: HMSO.

Home Office (1996a) *Criminal Statistics for England and Wales 1995*. London: HMSO.

Home Office (1999) *Preventing Robbery: A Guide for Retailers* (www.home office.gov.uk/crimprev/appr.htm).

Home Office (2000) *Criminal Statistics England and Wales 1998*. London HMSO.

Honneth, A. (1995) *The Struggle for Recognition*. Cambridge: Polity Press.

Hopkins, N. (2000) Corrupt police framed three for robbery. *Guardian* 13 July.

Hopkins, N. and Braningen, T. (2000) The great dome robbery. *Guardian* 8 November.

Hunter, R. (1991) Environmental crime prevention: an analysis of convenience store robberies. *Security Journal* 2(2): 78–82.

Jammers, V. (1995) Commercial robberies: the business community as a target in the Netherlands. *Security Journal* 6: 13–20.

Johnson, B., Golub, A. and Dunlap, E. (2000) The rise and decline of hard drugs, drug markets, and violence in inner-city New York. In A. Blumstein and J. Wallman (eds.) *The Crime Drop in America*. New York: Cambridge University Press.

Jones, D. (2001) Misjudged youth: a critique of the Audit Commission's Reports on youth justice. *British Journal of Criminology* 41: 362–80.

Kapardis, A. (1989) One hundred convicted armed robbers in Melbourne: myth and reality. In D. Challinger (ed.) *Armed Robbery: Proceedings of a*

Seminar. Canberra: Australian Institute of Criminology.

Kates, D. and Kleck, G. (1997) *The Great American Gun Debate: Essays on Firearms and Violence*. San Francisco, CA: Pacific Research Institute for Public Policy.

Katz, J. (1988) *Seductions of Crime: Moral and Sensual Attractions of Doing Evil*. New York: Basic Books.

Katz, J. (1991) The motivation of the persistent robbers. In M. Tonry (ed.) *Crime and Justice* 14. Chicago, IL: University of Chicago Press.

Kebbell, M. and Wagstaff, G. (1999) *Face value? Evaluating the accuracy of eyewitness information*. Police Research Series 102. London: Home Office.

Kelland, G. (1987) *Crime in London*. London: The Bodley Head.

King, R. (2000) Doing research in prisons. In R. King and E. Wincup (eds.) *Doing Research on Crime and Justice*. Oxford: Oxford University Press.

King, R. and McDermott, K. (1995) *The State of Our Prisons*. Oxford: Clarendon Press.

Kinnes, S. (2000) In your face. *Guardian* 10 February.

Kleck. G. (1991) *Point Blank: Guns and Violence in America*. New York: Aldine de Gruyter.

Kleck, G. (1997) *Targeting Guns: Firearms and their Control*. New York: Aldine de Gruyter.

Koppen, P. and Jansen, R. (1998) The road to robbery: travel patterns in commercial robberies. *British Journal of Criminology* 38(2): 230–46.

Layder, D. (1993) *New Strategies in Social Research*. Cambridge: Polity Press.

Leeman-Conley, M. (1990) After a violent robbery. *Criminology Australia* Vol. 1(4): 4–6.

Leymann, H. (1988) Stress reactions after bank robberies: psychological and psychosomatic reaction patterns. *Work and Stress* 2(2): 123–32.

Leymann, H. (1990) Social support after armed robbery in the workplace. In E. Viano (ed.) *The Victimology Handbook*. New York: Garland Publishing.

Lott, J. (2000) *More Guns, Less Crime* (2nd edn). Chicago, IL: University of Chicago Press.

Loveday, B. (2000) Managing crime: police use of crime data as an indicator of effectiveness. *International Journal of the Sociology of Law* 28: 215–37.

Luckenbill, D. (1980) Patterns of force in robbery. *Deviant Behaviour* 1: 361–78.

Luckenbill, D. (1981) Generating compliance: the case of robbery. *Urban Life* 10(1): 25–46.

Lyng, S. (1990) Edgework: a social psychological analysis of voluntary risk taking. *American Journal of Sociology* 95(4): 851–86.

Lyng, S. (1993) Dysfunctional risk taking: criminal behavior as edgework. In N. Bell and R. Bell (eds.) *Adolescent Risk Taking*. Newbury Park, CA: Sage.

MacKenzie, D. and Uchida, C. (1994) *Drugs and Crime*. Thousand Oaks, CA: Sage.

Maffesoli, M. (1996) *The Time of the Tribes: The Decline of Individualism in Mass Society*. London: Sage.

Maguire, M. and John, T. (1995) *Intelligence Surveillance and Informants: Integrated Approaches. Crime Prevention and Detection Series* 64. London: Home Office.

Marsden, J. (1990) Bank robbery: strategies for reduction. Australian Banking Association (unpublished).

Martin, C. (2000) Doing research in a prison setting. In V. Jupp, D. Davies and P. Francis (eds.) *Doing Criminological Research*. London: Sage.

Marx, G. (1988) *Undercover: Police Surveillance in America*: Berkeley, CA: University of California Press.

Matthews, R. (1998) *Armed Robbery: Two Police Responses. Crime Detection and Prevention Series* 78. London: Home Office.

Matthews, R. (1999) *Doing Time: An Introduction to the Sociology of Imprisonment*. London: Macmillan/Palgrave.

Matthews, R., Pease, C. and Pease, K. (2001) Repeated bank robbery: theme and variations. In G. Farrall and K. Pease (eds.) Repeat Victimization. *Studies in Crime Prevention Vol 12*. Monsey, NY: Criminal Justice Press.

Matthews, R. and Trickey, J. (1995) *Drugs and Crime amongst Young People in Leicester*. Enfield: Centre for Criminology, Middlesex University.

Maybanks, A. (1992) Firearms control: an examination of the effects of firearms used in armed robberies in the Metropolitan Police District. MA thesis, University of Exeter.

Maybanks, A. and Yardley, M. (1992) Controls are not bullet-proof. *Police Review* 25 September: 1786–7.

Maynard, W. (1994) *Witness Intimidation: Strategies for Prevention. Crime Detection and Prevention Series* 55. London: HMSO.

McIntosh, M. (1975) *The Organisation of Crime*. London: Macmillan.

McLeod, J. (1994) Cash and Carry. *The Independent Magazine* 15 October.

McLintock, F. and Gibson, E. (1961) *Robbery in London*. London: Macmillan.

Messerschmidt, J. (1993) *Masculinities and Crime*. NJ: Rowman & Littlefield.

Miller, S. (1994) Gun law. *The Job* 18 March.

Mirrlees-Black, C. and Ross, A. (1995) *Crime against Retail and Manufacturing Premises: Findings from the 1994 Commercial Victimisation Survey.* London: HMSO.

Mooney, J. (1993) *The Hidden Figure: Domestic Violence in North London.* Enfield: Centre for Criminology, Middlesex University.

Morrison, S. (1993) Both sides of the story: a comparison of the perspectives of offenders and victims involved in a violent incident. *Research Bulletin* 34. London: Home Office.

Morrison, S. and O'Donnell, I. (1994) *Armed Robbery: A Study in London.* Oxford: Centre for Criminological Research, University of Oxford.

Morton, J. (1995) *Supergrasses and Informers: An Informal History of Undercover Police Work.* London: Warner Books.

Mungo, P. (1996) A power in the land. *Guardian* 1 June.

National Audit Office (1999) *Handgun Surrender and Compensation.* HC 225. London: HMSO.

Normandeau, A. (1968) *Trends and Patterns in Crimes of Robbery.* Philadelphia, PA: University of Pennsylvania Press.

Norris, C. and Dunningham, C. (2000) Subterranean blues: conflict as the unintended consequence of the police use of informers. *Policing and Society* 9: 385–412.

Opp, K-D. (1997) Limited rationality and crime. In G. Newman, R. Clarke and S. Shoham (eds.) *Rational Choice and Situational Crime Prevention.* Aldershot: Ashgate/Dartmouth.

Ostler, R. (1969) The thermic lance. *Police Journal* July: 286–92.

Pawson, R. and Tilley, N. (1997) *Realistic Evaluation.* London: Sage.

Perry, K. (2000) Informant sues the Met over broken promises. *Guardian* 9 December.

Petersilia, J. (1994) Violent crime and violent criminals: The response of the justice system. In M. Costanzo and S. Oskamp (eds.) *Violence and the Law.* Thousand Oaks, CA: Sage.

Poyner, B., Burns-Howell, T. and Blakeman, A. (2000) *Work-Related Violence in Small and Medium Sized Business.* London: HSE Books.

Poyner, B. and Warne, C. (1988) *Preventing Violence to Staff.* London: Health and Safety Executive.

Quinn, S. (1996) Thirty per cent of boys 14–15 carry weapon. *Guardian* 23 September.

Read, P. (1978) *The Great Train Robbery.* London: W. H. Allen.

Reiner, R. (1985) *The Politics of the Police*. Brighton: Harvester.

Reiner, R. (1992) Police research the United Kingdom: a critical review. In N. Morris and M. Tonry (eds.) *Modern Policing*. Chicago: University of Chicago Press.

Reppetto, T. (1976) Crime prevention and displacement phenomenon. *Crime and Delinquency* 22: 166–77.

Richards, D. (2000) Symptom severity, personal and social variables after armed robbery. *British Journal of Clinical Psychology* 39: 415–19.

Rix, B., Walker, D. and Ward, J. (1998) *The Criminal Use of Firearms*. London: Police Research Group, Home Office.

Reuter, P. (1983) Licensing criminals: police and informants. In G. Caplan (ed.) *Abscam Ethics*. Washington, DC: Police Foundation.

Sayer, A. (1992) *Method in Social Science: A Realist Approach*. London: Routledge.

Seymour, D. (1982) What good have supergrasses done for anyone but themselves? *LAG Bulletin* December: 7–10.

Sheptycki, J. (1994) It looks different from the outside. *Policing* 10: 125–33.

Shoham, S. (1997) Situational aspects of violence. In G. Newman *et al* (eds.) *Rational Choice and Situational Crime Prevention*. Aldershot: Ashgate/Dartmouth.

Skogan, W. (1978) Weapon use in robbery. In J. Inciardi and A. Pottinger (eds.) *Violent Crime: Historical and Contemporary Issues*. Beverly Hills: Sage.

Sloan-Hewitt, M. and Kelling, G. (1997) Subway graffiti in New York City: 'getting up' vs. 'meanin it' and 'cleanin it' in R.Clarke (ed.) *Situational Crime Prevention: Successful Case Studies*. New York: Harvester & Heston.

South, N. (2001) Informers, agents and accountability. In R. Billingsly, T. Nemitz and P. Bean (eds.) *Informers: Policing, Policy and Practice*. Cullompton: Willan.

Sparks, R. (1992) *Television and the Drama of Crime*. Buckingham: Open University Press.

Sparks, R., Bottoms, A., and Hay, W. (1996) *Prisons and the Problem of Order*. Oxford: Clarendon Press.

Speed, M., Burrows, J. and Bamfield, J. (1995) *Retail Crime Costs 1993/4 Survey*. London: British Retail Consortium.

Squires, P. (2000) *Gun Culture or Gun Control: Firearms, Violence and Society*. London: Routledge.

Standing, H. and Nicolini, D. (1997) *Review of Workplace-Related Violence*. London: Health and Safety Executive.

Stanko, E. (2000) Rethinking violence, rethinking social policy. In G. Lewis *et al* (eds.) *Rethinking Social Policy*. London: Sage.

Stockdale, J. and Gresham, P. (1995) *Combating Burglary: An Evaluation of Three Strategies. Crime Detection and Prevention Series* 59. London: Home Office.

Stockdale, J. and Gresham, P. (1998) *Tackling Street Robbery: A Comparative Evaluation of Operation Eagle Eye. Police Research Group Paper* 87. London: Home Office.

Talbot, S. (1994) Armed robbery in South Yorkshire: an analysis of offences, the investigative process and the implications for national policing. MA dissertation, University of Leicester.

Taylor, I. (1999) *Crime in Context*. Cambridge: Polity Press.

Taylor, I. and Hornsby, R. (2000) *Replica Firearms: A New Frontier in the Gun Market*. Report 1. INFER Trust.

Taylor, L. (1985) *The Underworld*. Oxford: Blackwell.

Transitions and Trauma (2001) *Post Robbery Trauma Impact on a Bank* (http://www.bankinfo.com/positiveresponse/wound.htm).

Trasler, G. (1986) Situational crime control and rational choice theory: a critique. In K. Heal and G. Laycock (eds.) *Situational Crime Prevention* London: HMSO.

Viccei, V. (1992) *Knightsbridge: The Robbery of the Century*. London: Blake.

Waddington, P. (1994) Arming the police. *Police Review* 14 January: 16–19.

Waddington, P. and Hamilton, M. (1997) The impotence of the powerful: recent British police weapons policy. *Sociology* 31(1): 91–109.

Walker, M. (1992) Do we need a clear-up rate? *Policing and Society* 2: 293–306.

Walsh, D. (1986a) *Heavy Business: Commercial Burglary and Robbery*. London: Routledge & Kegan Paul.

Walsh, D. (1986b) Victim selection procedures among economic criminals: a rational choice perspective. In D. Cornish and R. Clarke (eds.) *The Reasoning Criminal*. New York: Springer-Verlag.

Walsh, J. (1977) Career styles and police behavior. In D. Bayley (ed.) *Police and Society*. Beverly Hills, CA: Sage.

Warchol, G. (1998) *Workplace Violence 1992–96*. US Department of Justice (http://www.ojp.usdoj.gov/bjs/).

Williamson, T. and Bagshaw, P. (2001) The ethics of informer handling. In R. Billingsley, T. Nemitz and P. Bean (eds.) *Informers: Policing, Policy and Practice*. Cullompton: Willan.

Wilson, J. (1994) Just take away their guns. *The New York Times Magazine*, 20 March.

Wintemunte, G. (2000) Guns and gun violence. In A. Blumstein and J. Wallman (eds.) *The Crime Drop in America*. New York: Cambridge University Press.

Wood, J., Wheelwright, G. and Burrows, J. (1996) *Crime Against Small Business: Facing the Challenge*. Bristol: Crime Concern.

Wortley, R. (1996) Guilt, shame and situational crime prevention. *Crime Prevention Studies* 5: 115–32.

Wright, J. and Rossi, P. (1985) *The Armed Criminal in America: A Survey of Incarcerated Felons*. Washington, DC: National Institute of Justice.

Wright, R. and Bennett, T. (1994) *Burglars on the Job*. Boston, MA: Northeastern University Press.

Wright, R. and Decker, S. (1997) *Armed Robbers in Action: Stick Ups and Street Culture*. Boston, MA: Northeastern University Press.

Yardley, M. and Maybanks, A. (1992) Caught in the crossfire. *Police Review* 9 October 1882–3.

Young, J. (1971) The role of the police as amplifiers of deviancy, negotiators of reality and translators of fantasy. In S. Cohen (ed.) *Images of Deviance*. Harmondsworth: Penguin Books.

Young, M. (1991) *An Inside Job: Policing and Police Culture*. Oxford: Clarendon Press.

Ziegenhagen, E. and Brosnan, D. (1985) Victim responses to robbery and crime control policy. *Criminology* 23(4): 675–95.

Zimring, F. (1977) Determinants of the death rate from robbery: a Detroit time study. *Journal of Legal Studies*. 6(2): 317–32.

Zimring, F. and Hawkins, G. (1997) *Crime is not the Problem: Lethal Violence in America*. New York: Oxford University Press.

Zimring, F. and Zuehl, J. (1986) Victim injury and death in urban robbery: a Chicago study. *Journal of Legal Studies* XV (January): 1–40.

Index

replica guns, 67, 70, 80
shotguns, 69-70, 83, 134
use of, 68, 77, 92
Firearms (Amendment) Act 1997, 79
Flying Squad, 2, 3, 15, 74, 105, 109, 122, 124-5, 126, 128, 137

Gabor, T., 60, 61, 63, 87, 99, 132
Genders, E., 5
Grandjean, C., 58
Greenwood, C., 77

Hawkins, G., 78, 82
Health and Safety Executive, 85, 88, 101, 135
Heaton, R., 123
Hindess, B., 38, 131
Hobbs, D., 5, 139-40, 144

informers (see policing)

kagoul robber, 16, 119, 120, 127
Katz, J., 39, 144
Kleck, G., 76, 79

Lott, J., 77, 78

McVicar, J., 7
Marx, G., 124
Maybanks, A., 72
Morrison, S., 70-1, 80, 91, 120, 138

Nicolini, D., 85, 87, 135
Norris, C., 123-4

O'Donnell, I., 70-1, 80, 120, 138

Pease, K., 58, 99, 132
Player, E., 5
Police Research Group, 2, 3, 13, 123
policing (see firearms)
dedicated robbery units, 104-5
clear up rates, 110-11
effectiveness of, 110-11
methods of detection, 114-20
use of evidence, 117-121
use of informers, 107, 108-110, 117-8

Poyner, B., 86, 87, 88

rational choice theory, 41, 55-6, 65, 90, 131
Retail Crime Survey, 98
Reuter, P., 108
Richard, D., 93, 135
Rossi, P,. 68
routine activities theory, 39, 131

safe-cracking, 18
Sayer, A., 12
security measures, 54, 57, 60, 62, 117, 131-2
Squires, P., 76, 78, 79
Standing, H., 85, 135
street robbery, 20

Talbot, S., 113
Taylor, L., 7
tiger kidnaps, 51-2
Tilley, N., 39, 131

Viccei, V., 11, 40
victims, 85-102
compensation, 93-4
distribution of, 97-8
gender of, 95-6
impact on, 91-2
race of, 95-7
repeat victimisation, 99-101
support of, 94-5
violence, 90-1, 130, 143

Waddington, P., 76
Walsh, D., 55, 74, 89
Warne, C., 86, 87
weapons (see firearms)
choice of, 67
trends in the use of, 68-70
Working Group on Commercial Robbery, 52-3, 57
Wright, R., 9, 68

Zimring, F., 74, 78, 82, 87